Longman Brain Trainer

ADVANCED

**Practical and immediately
useful advice on
learning and revision
for A level, GNVQ and
Degree studies**

JONATHAN O'BRIEN

LONGMAN

Addison Wesley Longman Ltd,
Edinburgh Gate, Harlow,
CM20 2JE, England
and Associated Companies throughout the World

First Published 1999

ISBN 0 582 36875 8

British Library Cataloguing-in-Publication Data
A catalogue record for this book is available from the British Library.

Set by 38

Printed in Great Britain by Henry Ling Ltd at The Dorset Press, Dorchester, Dorset.

Material that appears on pages 4, 6, 7, 31, 40 and 41 is taken from
Lightning Learning, by Jonathan and Brenda O'Brien, published by
Quantum Training UK Ltd, 1998

The brain and organiser cartoon characters are based on characters used
within *Lightning Learning,* © Quantum Training UK Ltd.

Contents

Introduction

Longman brain trainer advanced

There are many texts on the market that deal with study skills and accelerated learning. There are not many which explain in a holistic manner just **how** individuals can help themselves. It is hoped this will be useful as a self study text as well as a book that can be used in the classroom to help you, the student, learn the essential skills of how to learn. It is aimed at 16 years upwards, to be as useful for those with a mild learning difficulty as for those in need of more focus, confidence and motivation when approaching course work or exams, both GNVQ, A level and beyond.

What is the purpose of revision?

Is it just to 'pass exams'?

If you adopt continuous revision you will discover it also:

* increases/reinforces your memory power
* helps you build on the process of linking pieces of information together and using your wider experience to find solutions to problems
* builds on your overall understanding, general knowledge and life experience
* helps you learn to develop different strategies for different purposes, for instance, if you improve your note taking ability it will help with your record keeping
* helps you learn how to work under pressure and meet your targets
* teaches you to evaluate your own performance
* builds your confidence and self-esteem
* enables you to learn to organise your time to meet deadlines

 These skills are vital for successful study and will be useful in later life – they're essential life skills.

How can I make the best use of this text?

'So how can this text really help me?'

'Will it help me quickly and permanently improve my revision and so my exam results?'

The purpose of this text is to provide you with the latest knowledge on how the brain works to help you be more immediately successful in your studying. It isn't supposed to be a typical text on the theory of 'how to study'. It's written to help the student who is very busy working on a syllabus and who wants to study effectively without wasting valuable time.

Keep it beside you when you revise – it's useful to dip into. It shows you how you can learn to learn quickly; it will help you take control of your revision sessions in a way that will remove considerable frustration and anxiety. You will be able to choose the tips and techniques outlined here and use them in a way that will complement the advice you are given by your teachers and lecturers.

Some of the suggestions may appear somewhat revolutionary, some a little simplistic taken on their own. But try them out as a part of a whole brain learning approach and you will be pleasantly surprised! However, you must remember it's not a 'quick fix' for students who have left all their revision to the last minute. It is immediately implemented, though, and once mastered these skills will be with you for life.

 Remember: a small investment in time now, while you consider which style and technique to employ, will save you hours in the future. It could double the use of your revision time!

The benefits to you

If you know how **you** learn and understand the right techniques to enhance your learning ability, you will discover many benefits.

Tick those which most appeal to you

- ❏ Larger faster memory; greater success
- ❏ Greater control over revision sessions
- ❏ Improved organisation
- ❏ Improved reactions, speed of understanding and problem solving, especially in exams
- ❏ More 'free' time
- ❏ Greater satisfaction, happiness and pride
- ❏ Skills that you can use for life
- ❏ Increased educational and career prospects
- ❏ Less frustration
- ❏ Greater motivation
- ❏ Less anxiety and stress
- ❏ Heightened confidence and self-esteem
- ❏ An end to boring learning – more enjoyment
- ❏ Greater control of your future

★ Brainworks!

The comprehensive guide to conquering revision and exams for A level, GNVQ and Degree level

Answer the following questions to discover how much this text can help you **immediately**.

Did you know?	Tick	Yes	No
1. You can improve your brain's capacity by as much as 300%?			
2. You have two halves to your thinking brain and by linking them at the same time you will learn much faster?			
3. If you employ all your senses when you are revising you will memorise and recall better under pressure?			
4. If you work in a negative, pessimistic or disorganised environment, it will seriously damage your learning ability?			
5. There are conscious and subconscious ways to learn and you can double your ability to revise if you know how?			
6. There are many ways to make revision notes, and some will really suit **your** brain?			
7. Your sleep patterns, diet, level of dehydration, and fitness will dramatically affect your ability to revise successfully?			
8. A positive attitude and determined approach gives you an advantage?			
9. Timetabling an appropriate 'memory cycle' and managing it is as important as any revision and exam technique?			
10. Cramming is potentially disastrous?			
11. Water is essential to quick thinking and exam survival?			
12. All revision sessions should include asking questions, music, drawing, talking out loud and action as well as listening, reading and writing?			

Score

Yeses   more than 10 – your learning technique is sound; this book will help you refine it further

more than 5 – you've got some idea of how to improve your technique, but this book will definitely help

less than 5 – you haven't really got a clue, so read on . . .

As you go through the text:

- answer the self-analysis sections
- note down or use a highlighter pen to mark on the text any areas or ideas that especially appeal; there's a lot to choose from and you may not remember everything later on
- look at the examples of how these have been used by others in a variety of subjects; the individual-subject *Longman Study Guides* will also tell you more
- add your thoughts to the **action plan** page at the back
- stop and think occasionally just how you might be able to use one skill or another; how these ideas will apply to your own subjects

HOW LONG WILL IT TAKE? Set yourself minutes not hours but minutes not moments.

Part 1
Your Amazing Brain

An explanatory and self-analysis section that will help you discover your own unique learning approach and personality. You may realise you have been revising in a way that is less successful than it should be – it's rather like driving a car in third gear without realising you have two faster gears! You will find the improvements you make are generally rapid and also very stimulating and motivating.

Your amazing brain power

The more you understand your own brain, the faster and better you will revise. As we learn more about the brain, we realise we can use it to much greater effect. Your memory will expand and you will be able to control how well you learn!

We have learnt from the latest brain scanning technology that on average we only use 4% of our brain capacity in our lives. In this section you will learn how you can increase your **own** capacity.

Your brain is divided into three parts:

primitive brain
breathing and body-clock
heartbeat
sleep and anxiety

middle brain
emotions, moods and feelings
your long-term memory and your ability to learn

higher brain (80% of your brain)
it is made up of billions of brain cells (neurons) which are interlinked like a giant web. It processes thoughts, speech and all learning skills (but only when the other two parts of the brain are functioning normally). It is split into two halves or hemispheres:

left – 'academic'   *right* – 'creative'

The left hemisphere processes in a step by step way language, numbers, sequences, symbols, facts and procedures. It is more 'conscious' learning, logical and orderly and planned. It is information based.

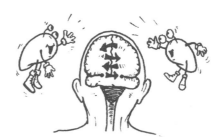

The right hemisphere processes in a 'whole picture way' artistic impression, patterns, melody/music, intuition and creativity. It deals with overall meaning and is more unordered and random. It is more 'subconscious' learning.

All learning should involve both sides at the same time – it is not enough to learn by 'rote' only using the left side. If you involve colour, pattern, creativity and imagination you will learn twice as fast!

If you are more dominant in one hemisphere or restrict your learning methods to suit only one hemisphere it will make learning, memorising and therefore revision and your speed of thinking in an exam much slower. So knowing how to use your brain in the way best suited to you will dramatically help you in your exams. And this insight can help you to learn better right away!

★ Linking your brain cells to make memory connections

There are billions of individual neurons or nerve cells in the brain (otherwise known as the 'grey matter') which are the pathways along which thoughts and sensations in the form of electrical impulses or brain waves are transmitted around the brain. These impulses contain information about your emotions and everything you think, see, hear, taste, smell and touch.

Imagine your brain as a massive road map with your neurons ending in junctions known as dendrites. When you learn something for the first time, a series of connections are made between your brain neurons; a new pathway is formed. The more times you repeat a thought or an action, the thicker the pathway becomes and the quicker a thought passes along the route. The junctions are given an extra coat of a substance called **myelin** which protects the nerve but also acts as an insulator and increases the efficiency of the nerve's electrical impulse. If you repeat your learning, a little at a time and often, you are constantly reinforcing your knowledge and are helping to fix it firmly in your long-term memory.

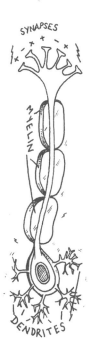

Why is this important to you now?

When you create a revision timetable, it should incorporate a review or memory cycle so that everything is repeated very often, albeit in summary. And you should use many different ways of revising to help create new memory pathways! Your memory is not just the number of brain cells you use but the number of connections between all your cells. The richer or denser the pathways are, the faster and more accurate your thinking.

Use your four brain waves to learn fast

To be a better learner when revising, you need to know how the electric impulses or brain waves can affect your learning.

Beta waves	The conscious/alert active waves when you are concentrating on work.
Alpha waves	The subconscious waves – often relaxed but focused.
Theta waves	These are deep meditation waves, which are very creative. They are most active just before deep sleep or before awakening from deep sleep. They are your 'dreaming' brain waves. Scanning over a topic before sleep can help you remember it!
Delta waves	Deep sleep waves. Your brain needs complete rest, so it is very important that you sleep properly.

We know that if you work when both Beta and Alpha waves are active you learn twice as fast. You can probably remember some TV adverts in extreme detail, yet you never consciously tried to learn them. Why? You were learning in a relaxed way! So wake up your waves when you are studying and create a larger gateway to your memory.

Knowing how your brain waves can help and by using the tips in this book to help you learn, you can focus on your subjects with greater confidence and increased memory skills.

★ **Your learning personality**

You may be a **skydiver learner** who prefers to get an overview of a topic, so that you can see the whole picture and where you're going before you start.

Or

You may be an **explorer learner** who prefers to work step by step as you go along, making decisions about where to go next at each stage.

Which do you think you are? Tick or highlight the items in each list that seem to describe you

*A **skydiver** begins with the whole in order to understand the parts.*

*An **explorer** starts with the parts in order to comprehend the whole.*

The high skydiver –	but –
❑ sees new ways of doing things	❑ can forget important details
❑ finds creative solutions	❑ can be disorganised
❑ sees long-term possibilities	❑ delays before starting
❑ sees the total picture – in 3D	❑ doesn't criticise ideas well
❑ is unhurried; doesn't worry too much	❑ doesn't stick to plans
❑ sees links between subjects/topics	❑ only works in bursts
❑ thinks of many new alternatives	❑ forgets resources (e.g. books)
❑ enjoys free-flowing writing	❑ is easily distracted
❑ has a feel for a subject	❑ doesn't file or rework notes
❑ enthuses others and is supportive	❑ doesn't often plan in advance
❑ uses lots of resources at once	❑ rushes into answers without thinking
❑ likes variety and excitement	❑ tries to do too much at once
❑ likes new experiences	❑ doesn't work out priorities
❑ skims through work very effectively	❑ leaves things until the last minute
❑ becomes totally involved in interesting topics	❑ doesn't check work
❑ tries new ideas and techniques	
❑ uses trial and error	

The intrepid explorer –	but –
❑ organises facts and materials well	❑ needs too much information before starting work
❑ sees links between ideas	❑ doesn't consult teachers or friends enough
❑ enjoys problems and their solutions	❑ won't try new approaches
❑ works things out well on paper	❑ becomes too involved in theory
❑ works well on own	❑ can be set in his/her ways
❑ is precise, thorough and meticulous	❑ can be impatient
❑ plans everyday work and revision well	❑ sees only one way of doing something
❑ sets clear goals and priorities	❑ is often preoccupied with details
❑ reworks notes and essay plans	❑ is not especially creative/imaginative
❑ isn't easily distracted	❑ is poor at inventing questions
❑ reads instructions carefully	❑ doesn't work well with others
❑ researches exam syllabus thoroughly	❑ task completion important – not quality
❑ likes to understand every aspect of a topic	
❑ works step by step	
❑ is good at finding and using resources	

One approach is not necessarily better than another it's just that your approach will influence which revision techniques suit your understanding and your memory. You may well be a mixture of both types – using both approaches. However, you will probably start with your strongest tendency.

Why is this important to you now?

If you know which learning approach best suits you, you can plan your revision sessions around it.

It is very important for **all** learners to:

- have a simple overview of a topic **before** starting serious studying
- plan a step by step approach to their revision sessions and exam answers

Your own personality will dictate whether the Skydiver or Explorer in you dominates. You will learn how to avoid the more negative characteristics. **Good learning has to be a combination of both**.

★ Intelligence and your brain

Intelligence quotient (IQ)

What do we mean by intelligence? Current belief is that you have at least eight intelligences and that they are linked to one hemisphere of the brain or the other: the more you use your whole brain the more your **intelligence quotient** (IQ) increases. This is called the theory of multiple intelligence.

Intelligence	Good at ...
Language	linguistic skills: talking, writing, reading
Mathematical/logical	numbers, systems
Visual/spatial	seeing how things look and how they fit together
Practical	physical activities: doing, building, sport
Musical	singing, rhythm, music
Interpersonal	communicating well with others, developing a rapport
Intrapersonal	self-analysis, positive self-talk, being objective
Intuitive	perceiving information not obviously available to our five senses

Emotional quotient (EQ)

EQ is your **emotional** intelligence. It's to do with behaviour, how hard you are prepared to work, how easy you are to work with, and the interpersonal and intrapersonal intelligences discussed above.

Develop your intrapersonal skills

Try to be emotionally self-aware; manage your emotions so that they don't control you. Try to achieve a balance. For instance, try to replace negative attitudes with positive ones and focus on self-motivation and self-discipline.

Develop your interpersonal skills

At work and school, the ability to understand the feelings of others is an important part of establishing a rapport with them. Try to develop your people skills. Learn to handle relationships with those around you carefully and sensitively.

Remember that interruptions in our emotional lives can have a marked effect on our learning.

 Tip – How can you link both hemispheres quickly at the beginning of a work session? Try juggling! Your left brain controls the right side of your body and your right brain controls the left, so juggling wakes up both hemispheres and makes getting down to work easier, concentration better and thinking faster!

Multisensory learning

How to learn faster and more thoroughly by using your unique learning channel!

This means studying a topic in as many different ways as possible to reinforce your memory. All information reaches our brain through our senses, when we are looking, feeling, hearing, doing, tasting and smelling; these are our **learning channels**. Your revision will be improved if you use all your senses when you revise. This is especially successful when you lead with your dominant channel.

★ Which is your dominant sensory learning channel?

Please rate from 1–3 in order of importance to you. (If you can't decide between one and another, give them equal rating.) The highest rating is 1 the lowest is 3. If you add up your total at the end, the column with the lowest score indicates your dominant channel.

We learn best when we are relaxed and still concentrating – that's when both Alpha and Beta waves are buzzing.

*We also learn best when we link both hemispheres of the brain by learning in a **multisensory** or **global** way using all our senses.*

I like to	Practical ('do', tactile/feel)	Auditory (hear)	Visual (see)
Learn	❏ Through **activity**, i.e. role play, drawing, by feeling, touching, having a go	❏ Verbal/oral lessons, lectures, talks, tapes, instructions	❏ Videos, slides, OHPs, diagrams, demonstrations, posters, photographs
Visualise	❏ By seeing movement, action in my mind's eye	❏ By hearing sounds in my mind's ear	❏ By imagining clear pictures or diagrams – accurate and detailed
Memorise	❏ By doing something over and over again – perhaps writing notes	❏ By repeating out loud, oral tests, audio tapes	❏ By imagining the topic pictorially or in patterns or diagrams
Remember	❏ By recalling actions – how, what was done, how it felt; actually remember 'doing it': experiments, demonstrations, etc.	❏ By remembering what was said; recalling the voice, names; using songs, rhymes, jokes, etc. as aids	❏ By picturing the topic/event; 'mental video': the way it looked, faces, images
Talk	❏ By gesturing, talking about actions/ feelings; prefer to demonstrate rather than talk; talk slowly	❏ By talking clearly at a comfortable pace, so everyone can hear	❏ By talking through images: metaphors, visual comparisons; fast delivery
Read	❏ More action-packed material, that involves action, feeling, doing	❏ More spoken text: dialogue, plays, audio tape; reading out loud	❏ More descriptive material, with illustrations, pictures, images
Spell	❏ By trying out the word – to write how it 'feels'	❏ By saying it first, syllable by syllable, sound it out (phonetically)	❏ By picturing in the mind
Total score	_____	_____	_____

Approximately 30% of all people are **visual learners** – images and pictures are primary helpers. Approximately 30% are **auditory learners** – talking and listening are primary helpers. Approximately 40% are **physical** – doing, touching, and actual hands-on involvement are primary helpers.

Identify your 'sensory preference':

Highlight which is the most typical to you

When I'm	Practical	Auditory	Visual
Concentrating	I prefer movement/ action; regular things to do	I prefer some light music, verbal explanation	I prefer to work without any music, movement, distraction
Inactive	I can't keep still, fidget, have to be 'hands on' to stop boredom	I mutter to myself or to others, ask lots of questions to stop boredom	I need to scribble, draw, watch something, look around, take in body language
Stressed/ worried/ anxious	Need to take action to correct problem; need a 'pat on the back', a hug to reassure me	Need to hear someone unstress me, reassure me	Need to work it out for myself; draw out a solution, picture/imagine solution
Relaxing – hobby	I prefer action – doing, involvement, i.e. sport, games	I prefer listening to music, radio, conversation	Prefer to watch others doing, plays, TV, read
Listening	I want to move, nod, gesticulate, physically encourage, don't want to listen for long	I turn my right ear towards the conversation, concentrate and repeat in my mind, think my replies	I'm impatient to talk, interrupt, don't listen always as thoroughly as I should
Making something	I immediately get on with it	I need someone to explain it	I need to see/read instructions, diagrams

You will probably find from the above assessment you have highlighted text in all three columns. Which type is most like you – which column has the most highlights? If they are all roughly equal, that's OK, but check it again to make sure. Can you work out a pattern – how do you learn best given a particular activity? Can you spot areas where you could now improve or develop your revision?

How is all this going to help you immediately?

Here are some examples of techniques which will stimulate the different sensory learning channels and make your studying more effective.

Taking notes – use space, colour, shape – with key ideas only. Use anything pictorial: cartoons, drawings, learning maps, flow charts – ideal in lessons, lectures and meetings. *These techniques are useful in all subjects, especially those that require summaries of large quantities of notes, such as History or English.*

Reading – learn to skim and scan a text. Check your objectives. Use a highlighter or underline. Use the punctuation to help you. *This is especially useful if your subject requires a lot of background reading.*

Memorising – use rhyme, rhythm, music, colour, patterns and your environment to stimulate reception, retention and recall. *All subjects can be reproduced in a visual/pictorial manner.*

Planning – take an overall view and break it down into small parts. Set realistic goals and plan breaks. Reward yourself. *All subject revision should be placed in a time framework.*

Audio tapes – listen and think about your topic and possible questions, perhaps taking notes or scribbling ideas. Useful for those involved in languages or subjects with a high factual content.

You may well recognise some of these revision techniques – but have you ever really planned what is best for **your** brain, considered what might suit **your** channel and the topic and the time available? At least four different actions are required to help encode the information. You may already have realised that the way you've learnt in the past may not have included all, but only some of those mentioned above.

See it, say it, hear it, do it!

Much of your learning to date won't have been multisensory, it will have only been directed at your left hemisphere (logical, step by step, listening, writing, linear notes). However, when you've learnt something such as a sport, hobby or musical instrument **informally** by doing, saying, hearing, seeing and visualising, by making it come 'alive' using all your senses, you will have learnt it subconsciously as well as consciously.

Advertisements on TV use your subsconscious – they appeal to **all** your senses, **both** sides of your brain. And you don't even know you're learning them subconsciously and off by heart. Imagine, visualise and recreate a mental story of an advert you've seen. You'll be surprised by how much you know in detail!

 *By using multisensory sessions you are using three memories – one **visual**, one **practical** and one **auditory**. You will recall faster and better. That's how you learn fastest and most thoroughly!*

★ Multisensory intelligences in practice

Remember that there may be lots of different revision techniques above and beyond those already mentioned. Here are a few more examples related to subjects to help you begin to choose your own style.

Art	Practise dealing with past topics; planning and producing finished work.
Design and Technology	Exam practice; use your visual memory to picture the processes you have been through. Use visual diagrams to remember the topics.
Maths	Define all the terms – prime number, square number and formulas. Make them into a game. Test a friend. Go through old papers.
Religious Studies History	List the main facts, ideas and opinions. Create spidergrams to link ideas together. Make them in colour, hang them on your wall.
Business Studies	Make a summary of each topic, covering events, issues and evidence. Prepare revision summary cards for each topic with definitions, business principles and applications, charts and diagrams, etc. Split into main topics, but create a brainframe to show overlap and links.
English Literature	Read the texts – highlight points in colour code for different characters. Make charts of evidence, quotes, themes, characters, plots, settings. Make a list of your common spelling errors. List link words, practice different styles and different planning techniques. Practise comprehension and reading skills.
Modern Languages	Auditory learners will learn by the sound of the words – record them on tape. Repeat out loud. Visual learners may need to picture what the word looks like, look for words within words *mal-heureux* and root words with different endings *nous voyons/voyions*. Use a highlighter pen, pick out the patterns. Try to make associations with similar words in English, équipe – equipment – sport – team. Audio cassette tapes are available with the *Longman Study Guides* and *Longman Exam Practice Kits* series.
Sciences	Look for associations, e.g. *photosynthesis* – photo = light. *Homeostasis* – 'home and snug' implies all is well.
	Invent stories, for instance to remember the parts and function of the kidney – 'My nephew (*nephron*), the regal (*renal*) and glamorous (*glomerulus*) Henry (*Henle*)'.
	Pick out words and facts to learn and write them on to small cards. Play a game with a friend to guess their meaning. Define general rules, e.g. Acid + alkali gives salt and water.
	Recall experiments by visualising the apparatus used. Make charts of reactions with implications – if it's heavier is it more or less reactive?
	Go through your *Longman Study Guide* and make a quiz using the summaries. Test a friend.
	Make a summary chart of all the topics, including definitions, units, formulas and diagrams. Make 'key cards' or posters with key facts for visual learning. Make flow charts of systems, patterned notes. Summarise important topics using headings like 'key terms', 'main ideas', 'apparatus', etc. Highlight key words and phrases, techniques in different colours. Practise drawing the key diagrams for each topic, making sure they are clearly labelled. Work through lots of exam-type questions.

 Choose whichever ones you feel work best for you.

Mind power

The right state of mind

Do you have firm beliefs about the way you've been taught, or studied in the past? These may have limited your learning capacity. For instance, you may have told yourself that you're 'not good at' French Literature, or Pure Maths – or someone else may have told you you were 'weak' at it. It could be, though, that you found it difficult because the way the topic was taught didn't match the way you take in new information best by suiting your dominant learning channel and approach.

We are often taught through lessons or lectures from books. These are sometimes academic, step by step books. This can be less stimulating. Those who are more 'right hemisphere' learners may have been put off a subject or subjects or even school altogether! Your beliefs may well have affected your behaviour – bored reactions, demotivated listening, no positive participation or even disruption. Then you're trapped in a downward spiral of gloom leading to eventual underachievement or even failure.

On the other hand, you may have very positive memories of formal learning – your favourite subject, a particularly enjoyable lesson, an especially effective teacher? Good results? Success? Why did you succeed – was it because it was more interesting, more stimulating, more fun? The chances are that you learnt it in a more 'global', multisensory way and once you found you could succeed, you began to believe that you would!

You can change the way you see yourself. You can remove or unlearn barriers to your learning success and produce excellent results that you didn't believe you could!

 *If you know **HOW** to learn, **WHAT** you learn becomes much easier, and you then use the power of your mind*

Positive attitudes lead to positive behaviour

There is evidence that optimists cope better in life than pessimists.

Consider these points

We learn approximately three times as slowly:

- when we're bored, learning what seems to have no practical use
- what we don't like and what doesn't match our learning style and channel
- when we're anxious, stressed or convince ourselves we can't do it
- in uncomfortable, unpleasant surroundings
- when we are tired, hungry or dehydrated
- when we feel negative and demotivated

We learn fastest :

- when we are relaxed, focused, motivated and positive
- using multisensory techniques, and through linking information with facts we already know
- using both Alpha and Beta brain waves
- when we involve all our intelligences, especially our favourite and strongest ones
- when we **believe** we can succeed
- when we have a good diet, exercise and sleep well

How you feel about learning is very, very important, because you will not be able to memorise or revise properly if you are in the wrong frame of mind. Above all, self-belief (self-esteem and confidence) in everything we do conditions our frame of mind – it is the route to success.

10 Part One   Your Amazing Brain

What's your attitude to a problem in the past?

You can choose to alter your attitude.

Think back to a subject or topic that has caused you problems in the past. How do you feel about it? Uncomfortable, tense, worried? Did you feel frustrated? If you can imagine the situation, you can probably **feel** the stress. Stress blocks our learning channels and closes down our 'thinking brain', it creates a barrier to learning. You can overcome this barrier by changing the way you learn and your estimation of your abilities.

What's your attitude to success?

Create a feeling of success.

Think back to an occasion when you have experienced the exhilaration of succeeding. Try to relive that success by 'dreaming' through it. Enjoy that feeling. What was your attitude? Were you relieved, happy, satisfied, in control, motivated, focused or positive? If you can imagine your success, you can probably feel the positive drive. Your response to this stimulus is positive. Your attitude to it is positive. It was a moment of excellence, recreated from memories. It's a good way of preparing yourself for a revision session.

In this way you can create your own **positive self-image**. It is a conscious act to place yourself in a positive frame of mind.

If you feel good about something, this will be reflected in **everything** about you. In the way you talk, your facial expressions, your posture, walk, stance, the way you dress, your gestures. You'll be perceived to be in 'success mode' by others. There is no doubt your positive 'aura' will be picked up by others and be reflected back to you. This will reinforce your positive behaviour and will have a very good effect on your work.

Constructive self-talk is a great way to improve your will to work!

Do you ever talk to yourself? Do you chat away inside your head? These are the 'voiced thoughts of your mind'. If they're positive they build us up, confirm our positive beliefs, they motivate us and are very constructive. If they're negative, these 'chats' are potentially destructive. Make a list of five positive things you can say about yourself. Pin it up by your desk and remember to talk through them with yourself when you need to improve your frame of mind.

★ Motivation

Motivation is a combination of inner drive, purpose, self-belief and potential benefit. It's often described as your 'get up and go'! Before you start anything you subconsciously ask yourself, 'What are the benefits?' Motivation is about a sense of purpose; it's an overall feeling of life control and focus on the future.

What are motivators?

Approvals	recognition, appreciation, acknowledgment from teachers, lecturers, and your peer group. Others comment on your progress and success.
Competition	with yourself, try to better your results. You may be competing with others in the same group, with an imagined peer group across the country also studying the same subject or even with the exam board.
Success	this is a general feeling of achieving targets, however small this might be. Higher grades, understanding something new, growing confidence and maturity of style.
Independence rewards	these are breaks, days off, evening activities, regular trips, visits and meetings with friends, a weekend to look forward to; the general focus is on having the responsibility to manage time and priorities to allow you more independence.
Consumable rewards	typical incentives are food, drinks, sweets: energy boosters.
Aspirations	goals and ambitions for the future. Planning short-term tasks, medium-term targets and long-term goals in life is very important. Future ambitions may include university, career, perceived lifestyle, wealth, happiness and so on.
Freedom rewards	this is when you are free to relax, free to work on something you like, free to move on to something new, free to make your own decisions about the future: which university course, what career, where you'd like to live.

How can you motivate yourself?

Motivation reduces stress, that damaging blockage to successful learning and work.

- When you sit down to study, dream your success and remember a time when you've been happy, successful and motivated. It puts you in a good mood before you start.
- Try to look into the future – if you work hard you will open more avenues of choice in career and lifestyle.
- What is your goal? – **constantly** remind yourself of what you want to achieve.
- Break your work down into manageable, '**bite-size**' chunks; it's less daunting.
- Plan your day – make sure the work, and the play, is timetabled!
- Be determined to do the work.
- Ask yourself, 'Why have I been set this? What's the purpose?' Find good reasons to make it seem worthwhile. You can help by talking positively to yourself.
- Set yourself sensible time-limits when studying, and reward yourself at the end of each session.
- Take a pride in presentation and performance.
- Find someone to help you understand work you are struggling with.
- Find someone who will praise your efforts.
- Look back at other successes, high marks ... and **believe** you can do it.

Your confidence will grow! Always remember your personal ambitions, they will spur you on and drive you to success.

Mind and body fitness

Essential to successful revision is your ability to maintain a positive attitude, a clear memory and a relaxed, motivated and focused frame of mind. To do this you have to look after yourself, both mentally and physically.

As you can tell from the previous pages, studying is not just about memorising – your ability to learn is affected by the state of your brain, your mind and your body. If you want to learn better, faster and more happily, you should look after yourself by having a balanced diet, regular moderately intense exercise, at least eight hours sleep per night and by working in an environment you're comfortable with.

★ Feed your body, feed your brain!

Eating wisely creates energy and increases your chances of having a greater capacity to remember what you have studied and of feeling less stressed. A diet involving plenty of carbohydrates is preferable.

Here are some hints to help you eat for your results! Your diet should include:

Don't eat your evening meal too late. You need time to digest it properly before you sleep.

- fish, which is often known as 'brain food', is very good for you. It also helps keep your muscles fit.
- food like bread, bagels, muffins and even malt loaf all include the necessary carbohydrates!
- plenty of fruit and vitamin C
- greens – these are packed with magnesium, which helps you cope with stress
- lean red meat or cereals and beans if you are a vegetarian – important sources of iron
- bananas – easily digested carbohydrates. Also a good source of potassium which is very important for stamina (low potassium often brings a feeling of confusion).
- water
- cereals – especially oats as they release a steady stream of carbohydrates during the day
- a light, easily digestible lunch – perhaps pasta, salad and fruit

> *Avoid*: *high sugar foods, artificial flavourings, fizzy drinks, and too much tea or coffee when you are studying. All of these will stop you learning well!*

★ Sleep

REM time makes up as much as 20% of our sleep.

Relax before you go to sleep. Don't become overtired by forcing yourself to work late. Don't cut down on your optimum sleep time, that's about eight hours. Sleep time is essential for keeping your brain in good condition for learning. The time known as rapid eye movement (REM) is when our brain sifts and sorts out information gathered during the day. Your Theta brain waves are active at this time. These allow us to subconsciously solve problems, or discover answers to puzzling or difficult questions. So sleep time is **very** important to your relaxed and happy life.

> *You will tire quickly when revising, so proper sleep is essential.*

If you don't sleep well try some of the following:

- exercise regularly, but not near bedtime
- stick to regular bedtimes
- allow some time to relax from your studies before going to bed
- avoid caffeine near bedtime
- listen to non-lyrical music
- get up and do something monotonous

★ Fitness and exercise

Exercise allows your body to work off tension, increase oxygen intake and improve your blood circulation, and gives your mind a break. Thirty minutes of moderately intense activity or fifteen minutes walking hard or riding a bike, five days a week, will do. Fit it into your daily routine: it will bring health benefits, reducing stress and the possibility of serious illness as well as helping your positive thinking! Stretch, warm up – run, jog or walk. Try hand/eye co-ordination such as juggling or throwing and catching. Swimming is especially good. Remember to 'warm down': slow down your exercise near the end and stretch your muscles gently.

★ Wake up your brain!

Here are some things you can do to help make your brain much more receptive to learning and link both your hemispheres before each session. Because physical movement stimulates brain function, you will feel more relaxed and your negative feelings will drift away. This is another reason why exercise is so good for your learning.

Go with the flow - drink H$_2$O

Drink plenty of pure water. Water is a conductor of electricity and your brain functions with electrical impulses. A headache and tiredness can often be caused by dehydration and your learning will be very difficult and slow. Drink a glass for every 10 kilos of your weight per day: it heightens energy, improves concentration and helps your learning.

Jump start your brain - to link both hemispheres

Your left hemisphere controls the right side of your body. Your right hemisphere controls the left side of your body.

Stretch as if before playing sport – march or jump on the spot moving your right arm with your left leg and vice versa about six times. It increases the blood and energy/electrical flow to the brain. Try drawing in mirror images with both hands, doodle identically with both hands or try juggling!

You will find that you can concentrate more immediately, that you can make quicker connections within your work and generally react faster mentally. This is because you have woken up both of your brain hemispheres.

Release the stress

You can switch off panic before every revision session and in exams. Above your eyebrows, on your forehead, are two neurovascular points. As you panic, blood rushes to the back of your head. By keeping your fingers pressed gently on these points, blood is encouraged to the front where your thinking takes place and you will be able to concentrate again. You can massage behind your ears to relieve stress too. If you rub and roll your earlobes you will listen and concentrate better! Some people do this subconsciously.

★ Create a happier environment

Your mind and your brain will function better if where you work is comfortable, safe, stress-free, well lit, of an average temperature, colourfully decorated and pleasing.

(See Part Two: Motivation and your working environment, page 18.)

★ Stress

There is no doubt that any form of worry, anxiety or stress will block your learning channel and dramatically influence your ability to revise. Your subconscious mind is reacting to 'outside' pressures.

Stress is a build up of tension, anxiety and strain. Everyone experiences stress and some can cope with stress easier than others but failing to cope is not a sign of weakness. You can train yourself to be better at controlling stress.

What causes anxiety and tension?

There are a number of causes – and what stresses one person need not stress another. Look at the list below. Tick or highlight those that have applied to you in the past.

Illness	Putting things off until the last minute
Being unfit	Failing to reach targets
A poor diet	Work mounting up
Low energy	Incompetence or imagined incompetence
People being annoying or demanding	Distractions
Peer group pressure	Interruptions
Bullying	Trying to do too much at once
Targets that are unrealistic	

Symptoms of stress

There are a number of recognised symptoms of stress. They can be:

Physical

eating habits change (eating more/less) • too little or too much sleep • stomach disorders • nervous habits, fidgeting • headaches • cramps • muscle spasms • breathlessness • crying • clumsiness • violence • nausea • butterflies

Mental

low self-confidence • guilty feelings • phobias and obsessions • loss of interest • lethargy • poor memory and concentration • failing to finish tasks • being irritable and angry • feeling lonely, isolated • hyperactivity • indecision • fearing the future

You may not experience all of these, but a combination of a few can be difficult to live with.

There are a number of ways to help cope with stress

Build up your own ideal 'stress tool kit'.

- Constructive self-talk.
- Increase oxygen input – deep breathing.
- Plan and organise daily routine, mid-term targets. Use a diary and have an overview.
- Exercise, diet, sleep patterns should be balanced with your work pressure.
- Predict the tough times; focus on your long-term goals.
- Listen to relaxing music.
- Give yourself credit when you are doing it right.
- Build in rewards – and intend to enjoy them.
- Attend yoga, meditation or relaxation sessions.
- Seek help – supportive people are vital, reassuring and great for confidence.
- Know how to say 'no' to those who distract or interrupt you.
- Smile and find people who make you laugh.

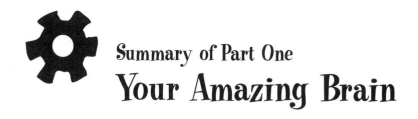

Summary of Part One
Your Amazing Brain

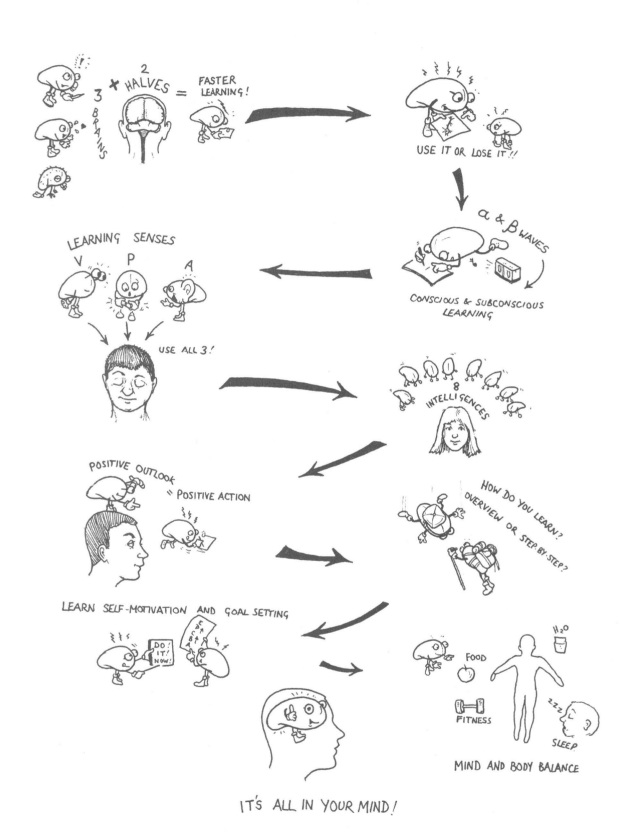

Part 2
Practical and Immediate Revision Skills

This section offers plenty of suggestions and skills that can be applied to any subject. These are explained in more detail in the Longman Study Guides listed on page 19. This text presents learning and revision in a complete programme that is easy and quick to implement. You can refer to it at any time.

Environment, equipment and resources

The physical organisation of your workplace is of the utmost importance. If you are to be in the right frame of mind, relaxed and focused, your workplace must suit your purpose.

15 tips to organise your workplace

1. You will need a room or area where you will not be disturbed.

2. You will need to be able to leave your work there **untouched** by anyone else.

3. You will need good lighting – using just one lamp can tire your eyes and lead to poor concentration and fatigue.

4. You should have adequate ventilation and an even temperature.

It's not the number of hours you put in, it's how you use them.

5. Your desk and chair should suit each other! The chair should allow you a comfortable posture. The desk needs to be big enough.

6. Wall space is very useful for notices, timetables, calendars, goals and so on.

7. Music is important, but only if it is non-lyrical and used as background. You should research music that is both relaxing and comfortable ... to help those brain waves buzz.

8. House plants add to the atmosphere – a bright and cheerful room undoubtedly helps too.

9. Ideally this area should not be used for anything else but work.

10. You should be comfortable and pleased with your workplace.

11. The facility to file away information, 'in' and 'out' trays and organised areas of your workplace help you to remain in control of your goal and purpose.

12. Tidiness is important. 'Organised chaos' is OK ... if it suits you – it can **look** chaotic, but still be highly organised.

13. Shelves are important, your work and texts are at hand but not on the work surface – think about positioning.

14. Adequate power supply is important if you need a computer or printer.

15. Positive statements on the wall for motivation – they don't have to be trite! 'You need a winning atmosphere for a winning attitude'.

How you organise your room and furniture is very important – your workplace should be bright, comfortable, stimulating and inviting. After all, you'll use it a lot, so you need to feel safe in it and like it!

Motivation and your working environment

Physical, motivational images and statements, spread around your work environment will help stimulate and remind you of your purpose and goals. They also create the right atmosphere to help you with your constructive self-talk and positive attitude.

Try using:

• photographs of people who are important to you and records of previous 'successes'

• certificates and awards you have won

• newspaper clippings

• trophies, cups, mementoes

• positive comments, praise and recognition from others

• favourite posters/pictures that give you a good feeling

• motivational slogans

They don't necessarily suit everyone, but if they cheer you up, use them!

Music and your working environment

When you are engaged in hard, concentrated work your pulse and blood pressure tend to rise. Specific, carefully chosen music can really help you learn by creating a focused, alert, concentrated frame of mind. Remember you have a 'musical intelligence' that will help you learn faster!

Music to work by must be chosen carefully. It should preferably have about sixty beats a minute and be without words. Music like this awakens your creative right hemisphere – helping intuition, creative thought and subconscious working. It allows the academic left hemisphere to become involved in conscious learning at the same time. But if it distracts you when studying some topics or subjects, **don't** listen to it. You'll probably need to experiment with volume too – too loud and you'll lose concentration. It will take some time to learn what is best for you and may require some discipline and self-control.

Many people listen to classical music, such as baroque music (Vivaldi, Bach, Handel). You could also try 'Relax with the Classics' (LIND Institute) or Mendelssohn Violin Concertos 1 and 3. For something more contemporary try Enya's 'Watermark'.

The 'kit' checklist

Your equipment

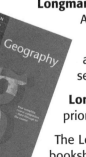

pens, pencils	calculator
ruler	paper clips
colours/highlighters	Blu Tack
ink	lamp/lighting
corrector fluid/pen	stapler
rubber	scissors
filing facility	glue
hole puncher/reinforcers	pen holder
folders/wallets/files/plastic wallets	blotting paper
in/out trays	printer ink refills
bulletin boards	dictaphone
paper – plain, lined, graph, computer paper	dictionary/thesaurus
dividers	adhesive tape
index cards/box	shelves/drawers
calendar	coloured sticky notes
personal organiser/diary	house plants
computer equipment; typewriter	pictures/posters
music system	charts
CD-ROM discs	timetables
brain boosting refreshments	

Chasing equipment is a great time waster!

So make sure that you don't decide to alter your room or look for equipment and resources just as your timetable says you should be studying! It's amazing how the mind can create excuses that help us put off hard work!

Really useful equipment

There are many study aids available to help you with subject-specific study and revision.

Longman Study Guides offer you help throughout your A or AS level course.

Longman Exam Practice Kits can be used at any time, but are particularly useful in the second year of your course.

Longman Practice Exam Papers are ideal for use prior to your mock exams and the actual exams.

The Longman study aids range is available from good bookshops.

★ Using resources effectively

This is another study and life skill that is largely underestimated. Having information that is relevant and at your disposal is often more than half the work. To make use of these resources will require some planning and organisation. Too often students rely on a handful of set texts to see them through and they fail to research more widely.

Typical resources include:

books – reference and text	photocopies and class notes
catalogues	newspapers
videos	slides/photographs
TV/radio	audio tapes
encyclopaedias	libraries and librarians
places	

And don't forget:

people – don't ignore them; the information they have is: personal, real, immediate, informative, often interesting and normally free! But make sure they know what they're on about!

computers – information technology, e.g. CD-ROM and the Internet. The Worldwide web is a source of information so exploit it if you can. These resources are often very easy to use because the instructions and skills are interactive. (But be warned, they are also potentially distractive too!)

There are other skills and benefits to be gained also: spellchecks, moving chunks of text around, graphics packages, better presentation, grammar checks, calculators, and symbols and colour.

What skills do you need when using your resources?

If you are a 'whole picture', visual learner you may want to get an overview first by watching a video before researching specific facts from books.

If you are a step by step, auditory learner you may want to interview people and put the pieces together yourself.

If you are a practical learner you may prefer to visit museums, experience real situations or try the 'hands on' approach.

 Make sure you combine all strategies and use a variety of different resources.

You should:

- decide what you want to achieve
- plan your time
- learn to skim, scan, and improve your reading techniques
- overview your resources and then choose a general resource to act as a template. You should make simple notes and then add to your notes as you scan each new resource.
- try to prioritise your resources in order of importance. You don't want to duplicate and waste time.
- add to your notes. Leave space, use colours, patterns and shapes to help your memory picture your research and ideas. Use highlighters or underline. Sometimes you may need a tape recorder or a camera.
- make a reference of your sources (you may need to refer back to the sources)

Organising time and mind

Time management

It's easy to waste time if you're disorganised.

Time Management helps you to do the things that **need** to be done, **when** they need to be done, in the **way** they need to be done! Being in control of your time is essential. If you don't take care to monitor your time, you'll find you are not making the best use of it. What isn't achieved in one day is passed over into the next and often your 'free' time is swallowed up in your efforts to catch up. This only causes stress, frustration and anxiety.

Time management enables you to achieve **all** your daily, weekly and monthly targets on time, and also helps you to attain your long-term goals.

> *It takes a small investment in time to plan – and it could save you hours!*

What takes up your time?

Tick the boxes that especially apply to you

- ☐ Academic commitments
- ☐ Work that has overrun deadlines
- ☐ Interruptions from friends
- ☐ Sporting commitments
- ☐ Artistic commitments
- ☐ Hobbies and activities
- ☐ Chatting
- ☐ Procrastination
- ☐ Extra work given
- ☐ Responsibilities/duties
- ☐ Research that takes longer than planned
- ☐ Emotional relationships
- ☐ Being easily distracted

- ☐ Parental demands/family commitments
- ☐ Poor listening
- ☐ Poor prioritising of activities/tasks
- ☐ Failure to anticipate
- ☐ Not planning day/week
- ☐ Attempting too much
- ☐ Too much detail
- ☐ Helping others
- ☐ Dealing with problems
- ☐ Lack of self-discipline
- ☐ Lack of motivation
- ☐ Illness/convalescence
- ☐ Worry/anxiety/stress

Once you have an idea of what could be wasting your time, it's important to look at how you are spending your time now.

Analyse your use of time at present:

a) How many hours are there in a week?

Total for week ____168____

b) How many hours do you spend working (include **all** work)?

Total for week _____

c) How many hours do you spend on compulsory activities, outside work?

Total for week _____

d) How many hours do you spend 'maintaining' yourself – sleeping, eating, domestic demands, travelling?

Total for week _____

Add b), c) and d) together; subtract this total from a). The resulting total is your unscheduled time – your **free time**.

Total free time for week _____

If you keep a record of how you use your time over a week, you may find you don't have the free time you should. You will probably find you are wasting time ... and reducing the amount of free time you have left!

Steps to improve control over your time ...

1. **Decide what is important** – not what others consider is important for you. What are your short-, medium- and long-term goals? Once you have an idea of what you want to achieve, you will find it's amazing just how you keep those targets in mind, especially if you have a diary or a calendar, or ideally your own personal organiser.

2. **Draw up your weekly timetable.** Fill in your important dates and commitments. You will know what time is already accounted for. Each month, week and day list those things you **have to do** and those things you **want to do**. These are your goals.

3. **Mark against each task a letter in order of priority.** Priority A should be those you 'have to do'. Distinguish their importance by numbering them: 1, 2, 3 ... Priority B should be those tasks which you can put off for a while (but you may need to eventually make them priority A.) Priority C are those tasks that have no urgency whatsoever, and probably never will. You can afford to abandon these or view them as rewards when you've worked your way through the list.

   A. **do it**

   B. **delay it** (if possible)

   C. **drop it!** (or use as motivational prize!)

   Now you know **what** is most urgent, and **when** you have time to do it. Occasionally you may find that, to keep motivation high, you fit in some C priorities. These are plans you may be looking forward to enjoying. It's all about balance.

4. **Now work out how long you need to spend on each task.** Remember to plan in overview time and review time. Break each subject into small chunks and allocate minutes to each.

5. **Enter your plan of action into your study timetable/personal organiser.**

6. **Fill in a record sheet when you have finished a work session.** Ask yourself – Could I improve conditions? How long did I really study for? Did I stick to my plan? How could I prevent interruption? This is your **time management sheet**! Keep this as a record of your studying, so you know **how** you've spent your time.

You can build up your individual pattern of study showing the actual amount of studying achieved and your thoughts and observations. You may think this takes time to do, but once it is set up it takes a few moments each day.

Another useful method of tracking your time is to **work backwards from your deadline!** The following is a useful checklist when using exam past papers or producing course work:

What is my final deadline for handing the work in?　＿＿＿＿＿＿＿

How long will it take to write, draft and check?　＿＿＿＿＿＿＿

How many drafts?　＿＿＿＿＿＿＿

How long will it take me to select information?　＿＿＿＿＿＿＿

How long will it take me to plan it?　＿＿＿＿＿＿＿

How long will it take to interpret the question/
problem and to initially brainstorm?　＿＿＿＿＿＿＿

What timescale do I need overall?　＿＿＿＿＿＿＿

★ Revision timetables

Revision timetables are an essential requirement! If you are in control, you will organise timetables already.

When should you start to revise? – about two months before the actual exam period. But, if you've been using the techniques we advise here all the time, you will have a clear plan of action already.

You need to know in advance:

1. Exactly what you have to learn.

2. Exactly how much time you have each week to revise, work normally, relax.

3. When the exams are.

4. How much you can **realistically** cover in a revision session (30–40 minutes).

 Don't set unrealistic targets.

You will need:

- a list of all topics in each syllabus broken down into manageable 40-minute chunks
- a calendar for your general plan
- a detailed lesson, revision session and free time plan – fill in when you will revise individual topics and build in emergency spare time!
- leave an hour in the day to be used as catch-up time – then you do not feel so demotivated if you fall behind and if you have hit your target, it's extra free time!

Example of timetables:

Memory review cycle

Reinforcing sessions

Look at the diagram; you can tell that if you repeat something after the initial session, you can maintain a much higher retention rate. If you revise a topic and then walk away from it for three weeks, you will largely have to start the whole process again. Look how much time you can save by building regular reviewing time (just a few minutes each time) into your timetable. It could be as much as 50% by using a better allocation of time!

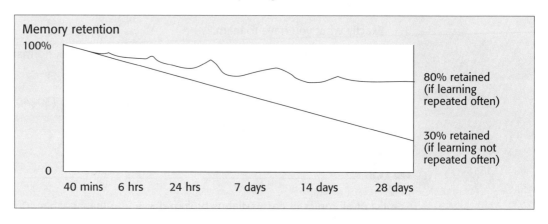

Memory retention

100%

80% retained
(if learning
repeated often)

30% retained
(if learning not
repeated often)

0

40 mins 6 hrs 24 hrs 7 days 14 days 28 days

Is cramming OK?

Some people seem to be able to do this – but are they really cramming?

Cramming means doing most of your studying in one big block of time, just before your exam. You cram it into your head. There are a number of reasons why this is unwise:

- fast in = fast out. It takes time to revise properly! Never try to learn new material the night before an exam!
- exam exhaustion: this is a sort of battle weariness. You're tired before you start, you may give your best in the first two to three exams, but then you slow down, subconsciously at first and then obviously. This puts you under stress and damages your results.
- when you cram you don't have an overview. You miss the big picture; steady long-term study gives you this.
- you should never do anything that makes you think less of yourself. If cramming makes you realise that you've let yourself down, this is bad for you. So try to avoid it.

When is cramming OK?

Cramming is more acceptable when you have been using a review timetable as above. You have retained 80% of the knowledge but you need to fill a few gaps. Cramming in this instance would be better called 'last minute filling'! It is essential that such learning is stress-free and not completely new information. Remember that repetition is what strengthens your long-term memory.

Here is a summary of time saving suggestions that may help you keep in control:

- plan ahead: timetables, priorities, know your task
- plan in: free time, rewards
- rework your notes as if you're studying
- use note-taking techniques (see pages 32–34)
- think ahead: what's really involved?
- file your work neatly **every** day; number pages
- read selectively (in depth, skim, scan) according to your needs (see pages 29–30)
- record how you spent your time – be honest!
- work with others, share the stress, ask for help

What is memory?

Memory is **encoding** ⇒ **storage** ⇒ **retrieval** of information.

All learning depends upon memory – without it **everything** we did would be a new experience. The more times we encounter something, the better we remember it, so constant repetition is vital to help us remember fluently.

How does the memory work?

You have a **short-term memory** which is the holding centre for about a maximum of seven pieces of information at any one time.

You have a **working memory** which is the action of repeating and rehearsing information.

You also have a **long-term memory** which acts as the permanent 'filing cabinet'.

*Did you know that 70% of what we learn today is gone within 24 hours unless you **intend** to remember it and **review** it. Look back at the memory review cycle on page 24.*

Messages are first encoded by your short-term memory. In order to retain the information, you have to transfer these messages to the long-term memory by rehearsal with the inner voice (repeating) or the inner eye (visualising) or by practically working on the same thing repeatedly (doing). This is why it will help you if you learn in a multisensory way and use all your senses to make as many different connections as you can. When you want to remember a topic, all the 'memories' that are associated with this information react at the same time to retrieve the information faster!

If the information is not rehearsed it will be lost or replaced by new information within seconds. A great deal still needs to be discovered about how memory works, but we do know that the more ways you encode to your memory the more efficient it becomes.

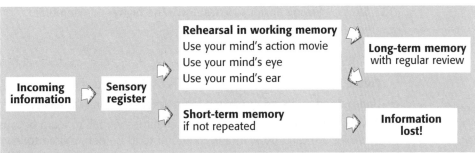

How to learn something new

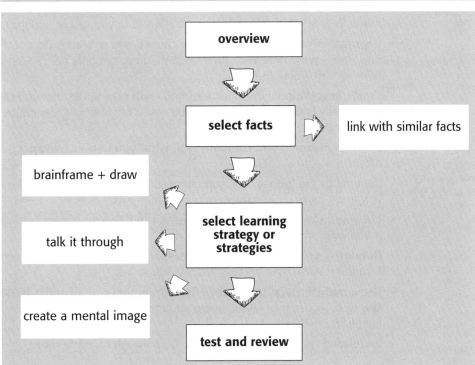

Why do we forget?

1. Poor understanding – your long-term memory will not encode information it does not understand.

2. Poor reception – poor attention, poor listening, lack of interest.

3. Distractions – when your mind is on other problems, exciting events, relationships.

4. Your physical state – tiredness, anxiety, emotions, mood and stress will interfere with encoding.

5. Interference – new information being confused with existing information; for example when you learn similar things together without proper consolidation (French Revolution followed by Russian Revolution).

6. Repression – unpleasant experiences (e.g. failure in a subject) will inhibit learning of that subject.

7. Poor learning strategy – not having cues or memory triggers to unlock and retrieve the facts.

8. Insufficient rehearsal or practice – to consolidate information you need a review cycle.

9. Lack of importance – you don't remember the unimportant (you probably don't remember what you had for supper last Wednesday – you do remember what presents you were given last birthday).

10. Improper organisation – trying to cram too much information into your memory filing cabinet without sorting it into categories.

11. Disuse – over time connections are lost.

12. Dehydration – the brain needs lots of water to conduct electrical pulses fast.

13. Stress – feeling anxious closes down the higher thinking brain.

Techniques to aid memory

- **Create interest**: find a purpose, 'This is useful because ...'
- **Understand it**: it's impossible to learn what you don't understand.
- **Positive thinking and confidence**: sometimes we fail to learn because we have convinced ourselves we can't do it. Intend to attend to it! Be determined to learn – avoid distractions.
- **Rehearse out loud**: speak the information aloud; create a script; verbalise. Create a story or movie in your mind (talk your way through it, to yourself or a friend).
- **Organise information**: into sensible 'chunks' and rehearse. Do not try to learn too much at one time – remember your short-term memory can only hold seven items. Plan in advance what you are going to tackle.
- **Create associations**: it's much easier to learn new things that you can link to something you already know, e.g. (carbon dioxide → car engines → greenhouse effect → trees → photosynthesis → carbon dioxide).
- **Look for meaning and compare with what you know already**: e.g. how do plant cells differ from animal cells?

- **Remember the 'unusual'**: if something is funny, strange, spooky, bizarre or even if it's vulgar, it's more memorable!
- **Put your information into categories**: it can help you remember if you can put it into a group with other information.
- **Develop a system of memory triggers** for each item you want to remember. For example, a souvenir will trigger endless holiday memories.
- **Use a multisensory approach**: employ a combination of audio, visual and physical strategies to use your visual, audio and motor memories. Make your facts varied and interesting.
- **Be relaxed**: play non-lyrical music to help the Alpha waves buzz.

- **Doodle, highlight, cartoon, underline**: use colour, charts, diagrams, drawings, brainframes, flash cards, posters. Hang them round your room to aid **subconscious learning**. Record ideas and listen when you are relaxing. Make key ideas and facts stand out.
- **Involve your emotions**: you will find it easier to remember things that make you feel happy, amused, successful and praised.
- **You remember best the information you receive at the beginning and end of a work session**. Try having a very short change in the middle of a work session to create a false ending and beginning to give your memory a boost.
- **Study for a maximum of 30–40 minutes**, then break.
- **Use concrete materials**: make a model or a game to represent the information you need to remember.

Learning strategies

Mnemonics – using the initial letters to create a sentence – Richard Of York Gave Battle In Vain = Red Orange Yellow Green Blue Indigo Violet (colours of the rainbow)

Rhyming poem – Thirty Days hath September …

Chant, make up a song rap

Look, cover, write, say, check (repeat and test)

Locations or room system – assign places/objects around your room to key facts. **Visualise** the room and the facts return too!

Number rhymes – for example: 1 = bun, 2 = shoe, 3 = tree, 4 = door, 5 = hive, 6 = sticks … By using words that rhyme with the numbers, make up a silly phrase that helps you remember numbers or dates.

The power of visualisation

Visualisation is a process by which you can make a word or story come alive in your head by experiencing it or 'living' it with all your senses.

For example, if you were asked to remember kettle, chair, banana, you may choose a strategy like repeat and test or remembering the first letters, but you would be more successful if you used visualisation and imagined … A steaming **kettle** and a delicious cup of tea. Sitting in a comfortable **chair** watching your favourite TV programme. Eating a **banana** split covered in hot chocolate sauce.

Test your visual ability

The rainstorm …

See the skies change - watch the clouds   **Hear the heavy drops of rain**

Hear the rolling thunder   *Feel the fresh atmosphere*   Feel them trickle down your neck

See the lightning   Smell the clean air

Taste the rain in your mouth

★ Examples

Here are some examples of the sorts of activities that will help to develop your multisensory memory skills taken from *Longman Exam Practice Kits*.

Make up chronologies

> **REVISION TIPS**
>
> **Draw up an outline chronology of the period. It falls into quite distinct sections:**
>
> ▶ 1914–18 Impact of the First World War on Britain
> ▶ 1919–39 Society and politics in the inter-war years
>   – Dominance of the Conservative Party
>   – Decline of the Liberals
>   – First Labour governments
>   – 1930s The Depression
>   – 1930s Failure of political extremism
> ▶ 1939–45 Impact of the Second World War on Britain
> ▶ 1945–51 Record of the Labour government

Taken from *Longman Exam Practice Kits: A-Level British and European Modern History*, p. 23

Make yourself a set of cards on a topic

> **REVISION TIPS**
>
> There are four main areas on which you need to concentrate in your revision.
> 1 Be familiar with the specific terms which are used in genetics.
> 2 Be able to reason logically from the information given to the required answer in solving genetics problems.
> 3 Have a thorough understanding of the processes and significance of mitosis and meiosis.
> 4 Be familiar with the genetic code, its manipulation and its application in gene technology.
>   To help the learning of **genetic terms**, make yourself a set of cards with a term on one side and the definition on the back. Each time you revise genetics, look at a selection of the cards and make sure that you can define each of the terms correctly.

Taken from *Longman Exam Practice Kits: A-Level Biology*, p. 15

Do past papers

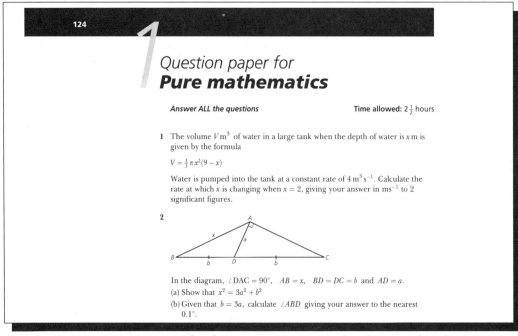

124

1 Question paper for
Pure mathematics

Answer ALL the questions   Time allowed: $2\frac{1}{2}$ hours

1 The volume $V\,\text{m}^3$ of water in a large tank when the depth of water is $x\,\text{m}$ is given by the formula

$$V = \tfrac{1}{3}\pi x^2(9 - x)$$

Water is pumped into the tank at a constant rate of $4\,\text{m}^3\,\text{s}^{-1}$. Calculate the rate at which x is changing when $x = 2$, giving your answer in ms^{-1} to 2 significant figures.

2

In the diagram, $\angle\text{DAC} = 90°$, $\quad AB = x$, $\quad BD = DC = b$ and $AD = a$.
(a) Show that $x^2 = 3a^2 + b^2$
(b) Given that $b = 3a$, calculate $\angle ABD$ giving your answer to the nearest $0.1°$.

Taken from *Longman Exam Practice Kits: A-Level Mathematics*, p. 124

Reading and learning

Successful reading means:

- being more selective when reading – this brings purpose to your reading
- improving your understanding whilst you read
- improving your understanding of ideas expressed in the text
- improving your ability to remember key points from what you have read

Before you start reading you should be selective: know your purpose.

The key is to read according to your need!

Ask yourself:

Why do I have to read this?

How should I read it?

What am I looking for?

You may need to choose different source material for different purposes:

Reading	
for **general ideas**	relevant texts and other media giving a general background to the topic, useful for essays or coursework.
for **specific information**	maps, graphs, statistics, quotes.
to **learn and memorise**	dates, formulae, vocabulary, facts.
to **critically evaluate**	an article, chapter, essay that presents a particular viewpoint.

★ How to improve your reading skills

Reading and learning is not about simply improving your speed, it's also about **understanding** and **memory**; the purpose is successful comprehension. Fast reading is no use to anyone if understanding is negligible. If you can read 250–400 words a minute – that's good. 500 wpm is excellent. 1000 wpm – you're a liar!

1. You must be **committed and willing** to improve your reading. Constant practice is vital.

2. You may be able to gain **an overview** of the passage or chapter by looking at the opening paragraph and the final one.

3. Don't follow words **individually**, but in groups. Use the punctuation to help you. Move your finger constantly – not from word to word.

4. **Avoid** saying words softly – **mouthing words**. This is called subvocalisation and really slows you down.

5. **Back-tracking** (regression/checking back and re-reading) often occurs when concentration and motivation are low and time is short. Use your finger, the punctuation and your commitment to stop you. Reach the end of the paragraph, then go back occasionally to check understanding.

6. **Using a guide** – finger/pencil or ruler can help you train yourself to read faster – but keep it moving. Practise daily.

7. Recognise **signpost words** (see page 41), underline, highlight, take notes (main ideas/facts only).

8. Placing **coloured transparent plastic sheets** (often yellow or purple) over the page often stops text from 'jumping about' or 'glaring' if you find this is a problem.

Reading styles

Learn to be competent at:

Skim reading   This involves a fast look at the book or chapter to gain a sense or feel for the text – to discover what it's mainly about, a general impression.

Scan reading   This involves looking for more specific detail by running your eye down the page quickly.

Detailed reading   Thorough reading of the text, if that's what you really need to do, i.e. after skim/scan. This needn't mean reading slowly, but comprehension and understanding is vital.

Bias detection   Reading to be able to separate fact from opinion.

Improving your concentration when you read

- Set yourself minutes, not moments, for your reading.
- Sit sensibly when you want to concentrate, especially if taking notes.
- Use different locations for different reading tasks.
- Have proper lighting (window, strong bulb, background light).
- Avoid reflective surfaces.
- Know why you are reading! Are you looking for a cause; defining a character; discovering a theme?
- Adopt concentration techniques – note; mark it; underline.
- Keep asking constructive questions – 'Why is it saying that?', 'How is this important?'
- Start with something easy to read – to wake your mind up, then read more difficult work.
- Every now and again sum up the main points, without looking back!
- When you have to read, be determined to make the most of it.
- Overview: general ideas (cover, content, page, index, headings, etc.).
- Review: if you decide to look further, look at the chapter introduction and summarise. Skim for key words/ideas.
- In-depth: read all the sections – skim any difficult sections to keep the flow going.
- Re-read difficult parts, you may understand them better once you've grasped the overall concept.

Use a strategy known as SSQ3R	**S** Skim	Check title and contents. Take a fast look at the pages to get a feel for the text. Look at the chapter headings, sections, illustrations and diagrams.
	S Scan	Look at the index. Fast-moving reading; eyes flicking across the page for key words/phrases.
	Q Question	Ask yourself your purpose; what do I want to know? Do I want to read it all?
	R Read	In depth. Find the speed at which you best understand. Try to familiarise yourself with specialist vocabulary.
	R Recall	Check understanding. Underline/highlight. Take notes. Test yourself. Have you fully answered the questions; is the argument clear?
	R Review	How have you done? What have you learnt? How can you improve? Identify and concentrate on your weak areas.

Listening skills

Listening is probably the most-used communication skill in the workplace. It is a very important method of learning. And you can be trained to listen – not just hear! Listening properly will save you time and it will also help you get a good overview of a topic so you record better notes to aid your memory.

Did you know ...?

- We listen in spurts – our attention wanders. Every 30 seconds or so, we lose concentration for a couple of seconds.
- We think four times faster than anyone can talk, so we can fill our heads with distracting thoughts while we think we are listening.
- We often hear what we expect to hear. Prejudice, past experience and beliefs influence our hearing.
- We don't listen properly when we are doing other things.
- We listen better when we are actively involved; asking questions, taking notes.
- If we have a good reason for listening, we listen accurately.

'PAY ATTENTION!'

Do you talk: at people? (you listen only to yourself), with people? (wish others to join in) or to people? (consider and respect your responses)

In a conversation do you:

listen and take in others' comments?

Just thinking about these observations will help you see how you can improve your listening.

allow others the time to speak?

interrupt – or stop people finishing?

use your body language (nod, smile, look puzzled)?

help the speaker?

How can you learn to listen better?

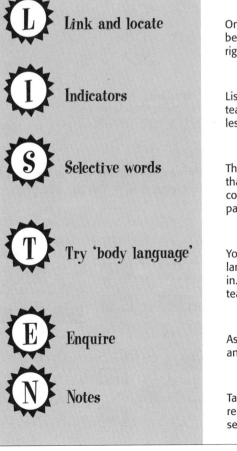

L Link and locate	On your way to your lesson try to anticipate what you'll be studying. Make yourself mentally prepared – in the right frame of mind.
I Indicators	Listen for the two to three themes or objectives that the teacher will introduce early – the main ideas of the lesson/topic.
S Selective words	These are key selected words to listen for: 'It is vital that ...' 'There are three reasons why ...' 'You should consider ...' Teachers will also signal these with gestures, pauses and so on.
T Try 'body language'	You can be an active and silent listener. It's called body language. Be on time. Sit where you can be seen. Join in. Show interest. Your positive body language helps the teacher teach better!
E Enquire	Ask questions – they clear up any misunderstandings and help you remember what you hear.
N Notes	Taking notes is an easy way of concentrating and remembering what you hear. There are many methods; see the next section for advice on note taking.

Note taking

Do you know why note taking is vital?

Note taking and making is one of **the** most important revision skills you need because:

1. It's active. It involves concentration.
2. Your memory likes simple notes in a spacious area.
3. It acts as a permanent trigger for your longer notes, essays and answers.
4. You automatically link both sides of your brain when you're taking notes – and double your learning speed!

Different types of notes

Brainframes

Also called mind networking/brain patterns/spidergrams/patterned notes!

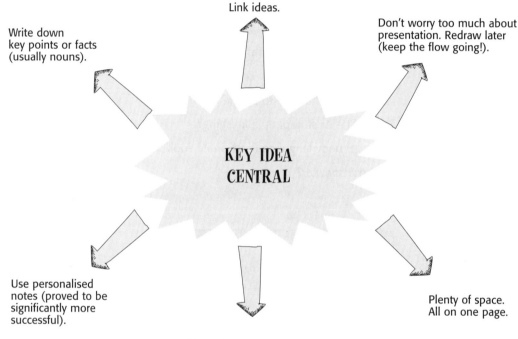

Link ideas.

Write down key points or facts (usually nouns).

Don't worry too much about presentation. Redraw later (keep the flow going!).

KEY IDEA CENTRAL

You can even create a brainframe of all your brainframes!

Use personalised notes (proved to be significantly more successful).

Plenty of space. All on one page.

Use colours, more branches, shapes/symbols to help understanding.

The advantages of brainframes are:

• Fast and easy • Hold a lot of information • Memorable • Memory trigger • Visual
• Can be used for any project • Simple to read • You can add to them

Diagrams

flow chart

fishbone

hierarchical

learning maps

spray notes

These are notes written in lines, often in lists and as 'bullet points'. You can 'number' each point in a variety of ways – but be consistent within each list. This is an example of one way to approach linear notes:

STEP 1
    i   Think before you start – only key points/ideas
    ii   Use label and title symbols
    iii Use your own words

STEP 2
    i   Layout/shape – don't crowd (add detail later)
    ii   Underline – central idea
    iii Edit: no full sentences, but don't edit too much
    iv Use diagrams/illustrations: visual = easy to learn
    v   Use shorthand/abbreviations
    vi Use colour: memories like colour!
    vii Use headings and numbers

STEP 3
    i   Link the points with arrows
    ii   Circles. Boxes
    iii Add extra in later: quotes; opinions; it helps you add another layer to your memory

Try developing and using symbols

- Use a 'dash' when you have to leave a word out
- Keep a wide margin
- Use a new line or branch for each new point
- Use only one side of the paper (space to add extra later)

Try your own shorthand

Can you translate these?	
@	//
&(+)	→
+	Ω
>	c.
<	≠
	pp
=	viz
%	ms
C20th	≈
∴	ff

Different kinds of emphasis

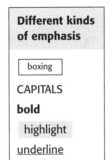

boxing

CAPITALS

bold

highlight

<u>underline</u>

A numbering and lettering system to try

- I, II, III, = main headings, then i, ii, iii
- A, B, C = points below main heading, then a, b, c
- 1, 2, 3 = less important

It's important to find your information easily so you need to:
- file notes systematically
- have a contents page
- have dividers and new files where necessary
- label/number clearly
- keep all files in one place
- keep notes neat: re-file occasionally

Summarise a process using a flow chart

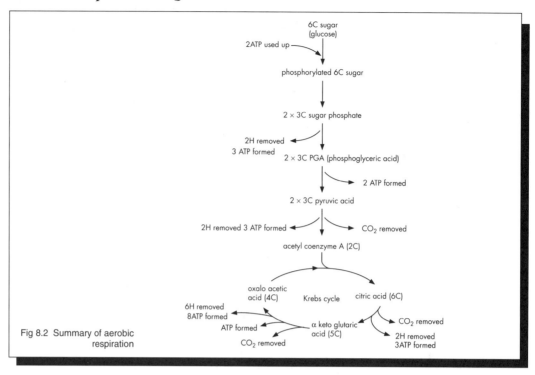

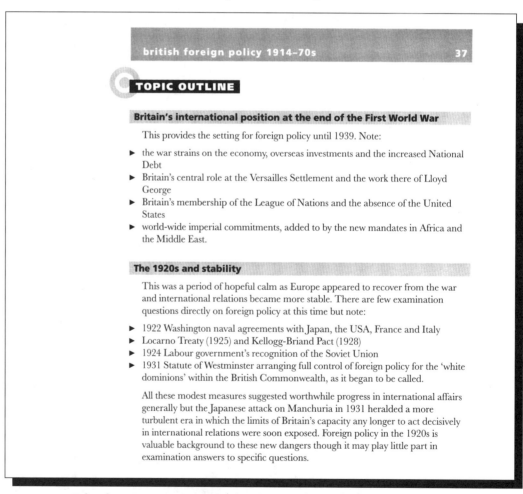

Fig 8.2 Summary of aerobic respiration

Make topic outlines of different aspects of a subject

british foreign policy 1914–70s   **37**

TOPIC OUTLINE

Britain's international position at the end of the First World War

This provides the setting for foreign policy until 1939. Note:

▸ the war strains on the economy, overseas investments and the increased National Debt

▸ Britain's central role at the Versailles Settlement and the work there of Lloyd George

▸ Britain's membership of the League of Nations and the absence of the United States

▸ world-wide imperial commitments, added to by the new mandates in Africa and the Middle East.

The 1920s and stability

This was a period of hopeful calm as Europe appeared to recover from the war and international relations became more stable. There are few examination questions directly on foreign policy at this time but note:

▸ 1922 Washington naval agreements with Japan, the USA, France and Italy

▸ Locarno Treaty (1925) and Kellogg-Briand Pact (1928)

▸ 1924 Labour government's recognition of the Soviet Union

▸ 1931 Statute of Westminster arranging full control of foreign policy for the 'white dominions' within the British Commonwealth, as it began to be called.

All these modest measures suggested worthwhile progress in international affairs generally but the Japanese attack on Manchuria in 1931 heralded a more turbulent era in which the limits of Britain's capacity any longer to act decisively in international relations were soon exposed. Foreign policy in the 1920s is valuable background to these new dangers though it may play little part in examination answers to specific questions.

Ideal revision

Revision work sessions

The ideal revision work session should consist of some or all of these suggestions:

Prior planning

- What time of the day is most effective? The morning is often recommended because your mind is not as cluttered with other matters and concentration is easier.
- Consider what you want to study.
- Plan sessions of no more than 30–40 minutes and allow 5 to 10 minutes for a break at the end of each session.
- Check you are choosing the right topic to be concentrating on at this stage, look at your timetable.
- Break your topic into manageable chunks – no more than seven main headings. Try to split each main heading into no more than seven 'bite size' parts.
- Allocate time to your topic main headings.
- Plan in overview time – what does the topic involve, how much do I know already?

This chart shows you why 30–40 minutes is a good length of concentration time.

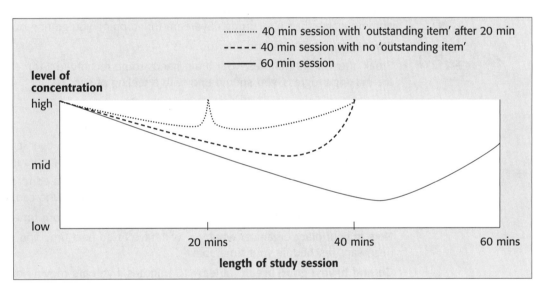

Work area

- Should be peaceful, with non-lyrical music playing perhaps – depending on what you're revising.
- You need good light, both natural and artificial. A spot lamp will help, but don't rely on this alone.
- Make sure both chair and desk match and you are comfortable.
- Have all equipment ready – especially your notes, questions and past papers.
- Put your session plan on the wall alongside your timetable and syllabus.

Brain motivation

- Intend to work! Fix on your purpose; dream your success.
- Drink some water and do some brain exercises to link both hemispheres.
- Relax, use relaxation techniques if necessary.
- Be positive and put yourself in a winning attitude.
- Plan a reward: an activity or pastime to look forward to.
- Talk with someone who is reassuring and supportive.

Multisense your work

- Decide on the various methods you think will help – read, recite, write, draw, highlight and so on.
- If you are attempting a past paper, use all the techniques you have been taught. If it is a timed question, stick to the actual timing and work under the same conditions as you would in the exam itself.
- Overview and then study each part in depth – focus on your objectives throughout; aim for precision and relevance.
- Half-way through include a mini break – stretch and brain exercise, perhaps think of something funny or bizarre about your topic; give yourself a psychological break (this is called an 'outstanding item' – see the concentration span chart – and gives your concentration a boost).

As you work

- Ask yourself questions: 'Is what I'm writing relevant?', 'What do I really need to do?', 'What is required here?' and ask questions about the topic/project: 'Who, why, what, when, where, how', and so on.
- Look for obvious links and comparisons.
- Occasionally move – stretch, massage to increase your oxygen supply.
- To avoid boredom and heighten concentration, alter your multisensory method.
- If you daydream ... dream it through quickly so you can get back to your studying. There's nothing worse than a recurring daydream for stopping you getting on with your work.
- Say 'no' to distractions and interruptions.
- Break after 30–40 minutes; your brain needs to be recharged. Stop each session while you are making progress, you should end with a feeling of success.

At the end of your session

- At the end, review your work for 5 minutes. Remember to go over it again later in the day for a few minutes, and again the following morning, to reinforce your memory.
- Be clear about what you have achieved – what else do you need to consider with this topic? What have you found difficult to understand and do? Who can you ask for help?
- Analyse how far you have got with the topic; mark it off on your timetable.
- Note in your diary/organiser what you will have to do next time you go through the topic. If necessary, reschedule your timetable.
- **Go and have a good break** (at least 10 minutes if you are moving on to a new topic immediately).

An active learner has a better long-term memory, is always succeeding, is happier!

A passive learner:	An active learner:
never	
plans objectives/finds a purpose	is in control of attitude and state of mind
considers other ways to approach work	concentrates on key points/facts
attempts self-motivation or self-discipline	summarises effectively
remembers much	uses multisensory methods
reflects on projects	applies skills gained to many situations
takes notes properly	sets priorities and finds a purpose
links ideas and concepts	prepares and plans ahead
sets time limits or deadlines	is inquisitive
always	brainstorms
copies everything word for word	records progress
allows interruptions/distractions	discusses work with others
works in poor conditions at the wrong time of day	takes notes well, using space and colour
makes excuses	can identify and interpret key questions
is late with everything	
regurgitates information without understanding	

★ Group work

Many people work in pairs, especially when revising.

There are many **advantages**:

- Improved interpersonal skills
- A sense of 'teamwork' and achievement
- Enjoyment
- Improved memory work
- Sharing suggestions, tips, techniques
- Gaining the benefit of other peoples' views; different perspective on the topic
- Teaching someone else is a great way to organise and reinforce your knowledge
- Extra motivation due to shared effort and time

There are also **disadvantages**:

- Choosing the wrong partner
- Using it as an excuse to play rather than work
- One works, the other copies ... so it's a waste of time
- Working together can be a distraction

Before you start you should formally agree your study contract – these are the rules that should help you gain the full benefit of studying with others while avoiding the pitfalls.

Define the task

Who, What, Where, When, Why, How?

Although there are various ways of defining the task and setting up the 'team', the general rule is that a co-ordinator (chairperson) and secretary (recorder) are chosen first. In the best teams these roles should revolve around the group, thus everyone takes some responsibility. It is best to divide the work amongst the group and agree what each person has to do. This should be recorded as a plan of action. Everyone should take responsibility for the task and for the group.

Create a plan of action.

Group workers can be saviours!

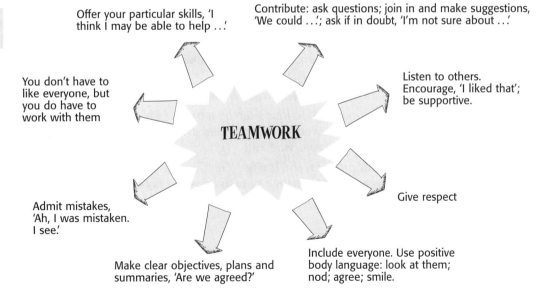

Offer your particular skills, 'I think I may be able to help ...'

Contribute: ask questions; join in and make suggestions, 'We could ...'; ask if in doubt, 'I'm not sure about ...'

You don't have to like everyone, but you do have to work with them

Listen to others. Encourage, 'I liked that'; be supportive.

TEAMWORK

Give respect

Admit mistakes, 'Ah, I was mistaken. I see.'

Make clear objectives, plans and summaries, 'Are we agreed?'

Include everyone. Use positive body language: look at them; nod; agree; smile.

If you are not careful group workers can be saboteurs!

- No one should dominate discussions • The group may rely on just one person
- No one should retire and let others do all the work • Everyone must pull together
- Antisocial behaviour: being late; ignoring others; teasing; interrupting; whispering; criticising negatively; showing hostility

Written answers

Subject-specific advice can be found in the *Longman Exam Practice Kits* and *Study Guides* – see the list on page 19.

★ The problem solving process

Producing a written assignment is very similar to situations where you have to solve problems in daily life, perhaps organising your holiday or planning a party or a trip. Your normal problem solving process would be something like:

1. Brainstorm – general ideas.

2. Collect information/resources.

3. Structure a plan.

4. Carry out your plan.

5. Check and assess progress.

6. Analyse success. Identify methods of improvement.

★ Exciting writing

To write well, you need to be creative and clear. If you can, try to write creatively, without much concern for criticism and without editing during the initial draft. Then redraft it. You can worry about technical detail later. To edit means to check, redraft, to be critical; we're often taught to write and edit at the same time. It doesn't always work because it can interrupt the flow of creativity and the clarity of what you **really** want to say.

Gaining and keeping attention and interest

*   Think about who you are writing for and what they will be interested in reading. When you write, consider what'll make them stimulated. Write for the reader, for the examiner.

*   Keep writing – keep the ideas coming. Don't worry if it's disappointing at first: take a break, come back later – sleep on it – and redraft. No one gets it absolutely right first time.

*   Make your first impressions really striking ones!

*   Write in a lively way. It must be clear and direct. Just because you have to write in a formal manner doesn't mean to say it has to be boring!

*   Illustrations and diagrams can be a particularly effective way of making a point. You should practise quick work for exams. They should always support your answer, not replace it. Keep them simple, work out a correct scale and label them properly.

*   Aim for precision and clarity – don't be vague – distinguish fact from opinion. 'Basically and in general people have a number of viewpoints on various environmental issues.' What's wrong here? Be very careful to write in a simple but precise way.

Imagery

It is vital to use your imagination to help the reader 'visualise' what you mean. It will help you express your ideas better, be more creative and allow the reader to be more involved and motivated. You can use this to involve the reader in a multisensory way, it's like a mental movie. Imagery is conveyed through metaphor, similes, personification, alliteration, onomatopoeia and other forms of figurative writing.

What do you know about paragraphs?

- Paragraphs are made up of sentences, normally several, following one theme or idea introduced by a topic sentence.
- All the sentences in the paragraph should relate to the topic sentence.
- Each paragraph should introduce the next step in the argument/topic. These should be linked in a logical order.
- Each paragraph should break the topic into more understandable portions and help organise the thinking of the writer and the reader.
- Each paragraph starts on a new line and is often indented to let the reader know a new paragraph has begun.

Some general tips

- Write in continuous prose or use bullet points, subheadings and so on.
- Use paragraphs to help you show linked points. Use appropriate specific language.
- Don't sound apologetic or submissive; don't sound pompous or arrogant.
- Keep it simple – write and explain clearly. Edit unnecessary vocabulary.
- Always sum up at the end.
- Handwriting/spelling: many marks are lost here; spell key words inaccurately and you don't impress! Credit cannot be given for what cannot be read! Aim for legibility. Use a decent pen and avoid cheap biros.

★ The discursive or argumentative assignment

This is the discussion of ideas, opinions and arguments with proof that supports a particular **viewpoint** – you need:

- an opinion; a view; an argument!
- evidence to support your argument – reliable evidence that is, not generalisations
- to consider all the sides of an issue
- to demonstrate convincingly – take care to choose effective and persuasive language. Words commonly used in such essays: to present; manifest; evaluate; to clarify; to demonstrate; to stress; to emphasise; to imply

Planning a discursive assignment

Draw up three columns: A = points for   B = points against   C = data/facts/evidence

Remember:

facts = evidence/data/information that can be checked
opinion = personal beliefs (not always based on proper evidence)

What's your opinion? List the reasons why you have that opinion. Show the evidence that backs up your opinion. List arguments against your opinion; can you respond to them?

Writing the answer

1. State your view (choose which side you're on).
2. Support your view (point by point with evidence).
3. Consider the other view (imagine your reader is neutral).

★ Writing an essay

We have chosen the word essay to cover advice on most written assignments because it is for many the most common form of assignment.

What is the purpose of essay writing?

Do you see it as a form of testing or is it just an assessment of standard?

Essay writing is a test of key skills: preparation; background data collection; planning; organising your thinking; testing your understanding; developing your powers of expression.

Of course essay writing is excellent exam practice and the comment from your teacher or lecturer will highlight important omissions, add ideas and also give you an idea of what you're doing right.

There are different types of essay:

narrative/descriptive: this relates a story or event and is able to narrate it in a clear and graphic manner.

analytical/discursive: discusses, debates, analyses and explains; often with evidence, facts and opinions.

Can I improve my essay writing?

STEP 1 *question interpretation*

Identify the key question words. What exactly is it asking? What type of answer is required? Focus on the title; read slowly two to three times. Highlight the significant words that tell you what approach is needed. There are some typical **key words** in questions that you should become familiar with:

Account for	explain and examine the main points
Analyse	examine component parts
Compare	look for similarities/differences
Contrast	set in opposition to bring out differences
Criticise	make a judgement of facts or opinion, through reasoned discussion and supported with evidence
Define	set down the precise meaning of words, phrase, topic
Discuss	investigate/examine through argument for and against; debate
Describe	give a detailed account
Differentiate/ Distinguish	look for differences between
Enumerate	list or specify and describe
Evaluate	make an appraisal of the worth of something
Explain	make plain; interpret the meaning of
Interpret	make clear and explicit
Illustrate	make clear and explicit
Justify	show adequate grounds for decision/conclusions
Outline	give main features/general principles
Prove	demonstrate truth/falsity with evidence
Relate	a) narrate b) show connection between events/facts
Review	a) survey b) criticise
State	present in brief, uncomplicated form
Summarise	make a concise account of the main points omitting detail and example
Trace	follow the development of the topic

STEP 2 *choose resources*

1. Collect your information: only relevant material (course notes, background reading, text books, videos, tapes, interviews, personal experience).

2. Produce notes – especially useful at a later date for memorising.
   Take your time: don't rush because the longer you spend, the more you will see obvious links and comparisons.

3. Organise your material and assess its importance/relevance – it needn't be tidy yet! Keep asking – is this information useful, how will I use it?

STEP 3 *plan your essay*

Produce a summary brainframe of your plan of action. Your plan will give you a more logical framework. Plans ensure the work is more readable and ensure that your attention is on the specific question and is relevant. This means you can time your answers properly in exams, and will help you create links and make comparisons.

Types of plan you could use: Flow diagram • spidergram or brainframe • columns (for/against) • storyboard plans • plan around questions – who, what, where, when, why, how?

STEP 4 *write it*

Don't forget you need to break up your essay into three essential parts: the introduction, the development and the conclusion.

Introductions	Rephrase the question to show you understand it. Define key words and indicate your direction. Set the scene; place the question in context. First impressions count.
Developments	Paragraphs (see page 39) Clarity: clear explanations. Organisation: linked points. Relevance: do your points relate directly to the topic? Personal opinion supported by evidence. Balance: enough emphasis on various points? – avoid unrelated questions.
Conclusions	Summary of argument, story. Suggest conclusions, tie up loose ends. Demonstrate greater depth of knowledge but don't introduce new information.

Draft: write freely – assume your reader is an 'intelligent layman'. Produce a readable copy – intend to rework it.

Check for: repetition, pretension, too much jargon, generalisations, unsupported personal opinion, poor paragraphing, punctuation and spelling.

Edited version: be self-critical! Check the length – too brief? Too much waffle?

Signposting: use signpost words to help you concentrate and link ideas in a logical way.
Examples include:
to begin: firstly; the purpose of this report is …
to add: furthermore; moreover; meanwhile; then
to illustrate: for example; that is; to clarify; for instance
to contrast: alternatively; however; on the other hand
to finish: to conclude; finally; therefore; thus; ultimately

STEP 5 *essay review checklist*

Have I:

answered all the questions?
covered the main points in enough depth?
made sure it's accurate?
arranged it logically?
ensured it reads smoothly?
used link words?

supported each argument with evidence?
used too much jargon?
kept to the point?
written clearly and to the correct length?
checked spelling and punctuation?
proof read?

★ Presentation skills

Just as you have a preferred learning channel and learning approach, so does your reader or examiner. You should therefore try to present your work in such a way that it appeals to different personalities.

A visual, holistic audience will appreciate an overview with plenty of diagrams, graphs and illustrations. The use of colour, analogies, metaphors and similes will also present the work more visually. A segmented reader will appreciate well-organised text: the skilful use of link words with facts presented in a consecutive order – perhaps using a numbering system – will make a favourable impression.

First impressions are vital.

All readers appreciate legible handwriting and a tidy, well laid-out looking script.

Here are some standard tips:

- use a decent quality ink pen or a roller ball
- your paragraphs and sentences should not be too long
- vary your presentation according to subjects
- incorporate where appropriate pie charts, charts, logs, bar graphs, diagrams, sketches, annotated maps

> *'A picture is worth a thousand words' because the eye and the brain create the visual memory that is **so** important*

Ways of varying the presentation without using diagrams or illustrations are:

- using bullet points or asterisks
- using headings and subheadings
- shading
- changing your font: use *italics*, **bold** or CAPITAL LETTERS
- laying out examples and quotes in a different and attractive way

Above all – try to make your work look attractive!

> *Follow a logical pattern and remember to keep it simple – you can actually make the text harder to read if you introduce too much variety.*

Different types of questions

The questions that will be used to test you come in many different forms: from a multiple choice question that will take seconds to answer to a 45-minute essay. These guidelines on tackling different types of exam questions are all taken from *A-Level Longman Exam Practice Kits*.

★ Tackling a structured question in chemistry

Structured questions

A structured question consists of a number of parts, usually labelled (a), (b), (c), etc. A part may be subdivided into parts labelled (i), (ii), (iii), etc. Each part usually requires a short answer and the marks allocated to it are shown alongside the lines or space for the answer. Although you may often judge from the lines or space how much to write, you may sometimes be given a whole line for just a one-word answer. *Always use the marks to check how much time to spend on each part*.

When one part of a question is further divided into parts, the subdivisions (a)(i), (a)(ii), (a)(iii), etc., are usually linked together so that one part leads you on to the next. If these parts involve a calculation, they may lead you through the working in easy stages. Sometimes, **but not always**, a structured question is a stepped question in which successive parts become progressively more difficult. *Always quickly scan through an entire structured question before you tackle any of its parts*.

When one part of a question is worth two or more marks, you know that your answer must contain two or more points worth one mark each. However, sometimes your answer must contain two points for one mark: e.g. a correct numerical answer *without* the units may earn you no marks. And even with the correct units, your numerical answer might earn no marks if the number of significant figures is incorrect. So beware – examiners do not give half marks! *Always make sure that your answers are complete and appropriate*.

A structured question (or one of its parts) may begin with some data or information needed to answer some or all of the parts. You will see examples of this in Part II and Part IV of this book. Relative atomic mass (r.a.m.) values are often needed in a calculation. Examination boards may include them in a Periodic Table provided for the papers. They may also print these r.a.m. values on the front of the examination paper or, as we have done, at an appropriate place in the question. The data and information could give you strong clues to the examiner's thinking and the answer required. *Always check the information provided and make appropriate use of the data supplied*.

Taken from *Longman Exam Practice Kits: A-Level Chemistry*, p. 3

Document questions

These commonly occupy half of one of the two A-level examination papers and, although questions differ between boards, a pattern of sub-questions usually runs from year to year. It is almost invariably sensible to answer the document questions before any essay questions. Considerable concentration is required to read through the extracts at speed and each of the sub-questions requires a new start: the complexity of all this is best faced when fresh at the beginning of the examination.

Patterns of sub-questions

You need to familiarize yourself with the pattern of sub-questions used by your examination board; a common one for 25 marks is:

(a) simply identifying a term or people referred to in the documents *(2 marks)*
(b) explaining the argument in one of the documents *(4 marks)*
(c) comparing the evidence in one document with that in another or discussing how far the two documents agree with each other on some issue *(4 marks)*
(d) describing in what ways the language (and the tone) of one document promote the author's purpose *(4 marks)*
(e) noting the origins of one (or more) document(s) and explaining why a historian might consider it to be of value and yet wish to treat it with caution *(4 marks)*
(f) using the evidence in these documents and your own knowledge to explain why . . . *(7 marks)*

An alternative (f) might read 'From your own knowledge examine how full an account of (the topic) can be constructed from **the evidence in** these documents', which involves explaining what of value is in the documents for this purpose and then, from your own knowledge, indicating what is not there or there only in an unsatisfactory form. Note here the words which I have put in bold print and which make it clear that it is the content of the document and not its origins with which you are concerned.

In answering document questions:

▶ Relate the amount you write to the mark tariff on offer . . . a word or two for 1 mark, a paragraph for 4 marks and a page for 7 marks is a simple rule, but be a bit flexible.

▶ Read the documents quickly before you start so that you have the overall feel of what their range is and what the issues are.

▶ Try to cite evidence in the documents which supports your analysis but do this briefly; it is *not* usually enough just to refer to the numbers of the lines in the documents.

▶ Despite all the complexity try not to exceed the time allowed for the question. If there are two document and two essay questions in three hours and each is worth 25 marks then the time available is 45 minutes. Try (very hard indeed) in these circumstances not to go beyond 50 minutes, at the most, for each of the document questions.

Despite this advice you are unlikely to do well unless you have had extensive document question practice, some of it under timed conditions, prior to the examination. If, during your course, this practice has been neglected then some of your revision time should be spent on it. The examination is not competitive so this could be an ideal opportunity to do some group revision to everyone's benefit.

Taken from *Longman Exam Practice Kits: A-Level British and European Modern History*, pp. 4–5

★ Some of the question types you may find in physics

Multiple choice tests

The most common form of multiple choice question is one which consists of a short statement which is to be completed by selecting one of five responses. Only one of the responses is correct and the others are called distractors. These are designed to trap candidates making commonly occurring errors. But there are other types such as the multiple completion type where you have first to decide whether each of, usually, three statements is correct and then choose an answer which corresponds to the correct combination of statements. Normally about forty questions need to be completed in an hour and a half. Multiple choice questions are very good for doing revision even if there will be none in your exam because they can help you find out quickly whether you have understood the topic. Remember you can learn as much from your mistakes as from your correct responses. This book contains a small number of questions of this type. If you find these useful in your revision remember that you can find more in the *Longman A-Level Study Guide*.

Comprehension questions

It is quite common for a comprehension or passage analysis test to be set, the aim being to find out about your communication skills and the way you can apply the concepts you have learned in your course. A passage, sometimes edited from a scientific text, is presented. As well as having to show whether you know enough physics to follow the author's ideas, you may be asked some questions about the consequences of the ideas or you may have to suggest alternative methods or strategies to those in the passage.

If you are to face questions of this type try to get some past examples. Read through the text of one of your examples at a reasonable normal reading speed in order to get an overview of what it is about. Then work through the set questions in order. Where necessary refer back to the passage for greater comprehension and avoid quoting the passage back to the examiners when you are trying to put the answer into your own words. With each question you may find it useful to jot down on rough paper any formulae which may seem applicable. Aim for clear and concise answers which use your knowledge of physics. Don't be tempted to write long rambling sentences. It is common to find that as you get toward the end of the test your understanding increases to a point where you notice mistakes in the answers you had written first. You can then go back and correct these.

Practical tests and data analysis questions

Unless your experimental work is examined by a form of continuous assessment, it is likely that part of your examination will be a practical test. The types of test used by A-Level boards vary considerably. Some boards set a data analysis question where candidates are provided with some data from an experiment already carried out which they must analyse.

Taken from *Longman Exam Practice Kit: A-Level Physics*, p. 4

★ Approaching an essay question in history

Essay questions

The standard challenge set by the examiners is for the candidate to complete four essay answers in three hours and this usually accounts for half the marks in the A-level history examination:

► each question is usually marked out of 25.
► grade boundaries can vary marginally from year to year depending for example on the examiners' assessment of the difficulty of the paper in the light of the answers from candidates.

Essay marks

► The normal pass (bottom E grade) mark for an essay will be 10.
► Four marks each worth 15 will give a B grade.
► The most interesting marks for an essay under this scheme of marking are 15 and 16.
► A mark of 15 will have lots of historical information and, equally important, a number of comments which relate to the terms of the question set. The answer may well tell the story of what happened but the comments raise this into a relevant answer to the problem or issue posed in the question.
► Marks down from 15 will have fewer comments until, at around 11 and 12 marks, they simply give an account of what happened with the terms of the question forgotten.
► Below 11 the account will have errors, gaps and irrelevant passages and, with enough of these weaknesses, will fail to reach A-level standard.
► The mark of 16 indicates that the candidate has risen above just telling the story and commenting but has seen that there is an issue involved in the question and has tried to provide a directly argued or analytical answer. Such an answer rises above the historical information the candidate has available and the factual knowledge becomes the servant of the answer. The chronological historical narrative is abandoned and historical information is organized in support of an argument or analysis.
► The higher marks above 16 will go to analytical or argued answers which are particularly well constructed, particularly well supported by sound knowledge or contain especially perceptive insights. These answers have, however, got to this position only because they are, above all, direct answers set in the terms of the question.
► Candidates wanting an A grade will need to be able to produce the 16 or 16+ answer. How to do this cannot be learned just in the pre-examination revision time, though an awareness of what is needed at this high level may greatly improve the able candidate's chances of an A grade.
► For other candidates there is a simpler message that, in the narrative essays which most of us write, explaining what happened, the more and better comments you can make which tie the narrative into the question, the better your prospects of getting a B or C grade.

Taken from *Longman Exam Practice Kit: A-Level British and European Modern History*, p. 5

Practical and Immediate Revision Skills

Consider how best to revise a subject or topic. Ask yourself:

- What do I know already?
- What do I need to know?

CREATE A POSITIVE WORKPLACE

COLLECT EQUIPMENT

COLLECT RESOURCES

WATCH THE TIME - WHERE DOES IT GO?

PRIORITISE

TIMETABLE!

MONTH WEEK DAY

MULTI-SENSE

SEE IT!

SAY IT!

DO IT!

INFORMATION

TAKE NOTES. REVIEW REGULARLY.

READ - SQ3R
SKIM
QUESTION
READ
RECALL
REVIEW

WORK IN PARTNERSHIP - IF YOU CAN!

WHOLE BRAIN LEARNING

H_2O DRINK WATER

EXERCISE

40 MINUTES THEN BREAK!

THE IDEAL LEARNING SESSION.

Part 3
Practical Exam Skills

This section allows you the opportunity to choose the best approach to your exams. It has many practical tips to help you with your exams. Once again you can dip in and out of it, but it will be more effective if you can combine it with Part One and Part Two to form an on-going strategy for success.

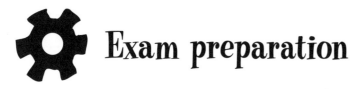

Exam preparation

Exam preparation is a little different from straightforward revision – it's about how you cope with your studies in the days and weeks actually running up to the exam.

★ Active revision

Here is a 'quick fire' review to consider:

- Consider how best to revise from specific types of material (essays, class notes, tapes, etc.). Use different methods of revision.
- Use reference or index cards to summarise main points, facts, ideas, sketch answers.
- Work for 30–40 minutes, then break.
- Revise topic three to four times and review general points often.
- Revise at a sensible time of day.
- Don't leave out topics – unless advised by your teacher.
- Use past papers: refer to *Longman Study Guides*, *Exam Practice Kits* and *Practice Exam Papers*.
- Look at typical questions – the number, choice or compulsory, mark allocation and time allowed.

★ Memory work

Use the techniques which stimulate your memory:

- intend to remember
- visualise – create a mental image of the information
- focus on key points/words only
- use simple plans (brainframes)
- devise a colour code
- identify typical questions
- plan your review cycle (see pages 24, 25 and 36 and below)
- work towards sketch answers; try to do this under exam conditions – 'unseen'
- finally review by adding extra information, colour over, illustrate and add new quotes

Review cycle

- skim/scan read; concentrate for a few focused seconds
- talk through key points in your head
- review for 35–40 minutes then take a break to recharge your energy and concentration
- learn – intend to learn from notes
- test yourself at the end
- review the topic for 5 minutes in the evening
- review again for 5 minutes in the early morning

★ Answering questions

Before you start answering or revising a topic question, ask yourself ...

What's my purpose? What's wanted? Is it an essay/report/summary/article/letter/plan? Look at the question command words and guide words.

What is the expected content? How long should the answer be? What do I include? What do I leave out? What is the timescale? Which resources?

Who is the audience? What does the examiner expect?

How is it best produced? Which style? Which presentation?

★ Past paper questions

Working with past paper questions is excellent preparation for the real exam.

You should aim to:

- overview – can you spot 'typical question trends'?
- produce answer plans on general topics and also on more specific areas.
- practise introductions and conclusions
- check you are using an appropriate style
- make sure you are using the right supporting evidence
- choose relevant quotes
- practise timing answers and proof reading

★ The evening before the exam

- Check all equipment/supplies
- Finish intense work by 8 p.m.
- Exercise – work off stress (run, walk, swim, vigorous exercise)

Evening timetable

9.00 p.m.	Review all topics for the next day's exam
9.40	Have plenty of relaxation. Try to clear your mind and be cheerful!
10.30	Overview your topics
c 11.00	Sleep (you need eight hours)

★ Morning of the exam

- Rise early – allow yourself time to do all the things you need to without rushing yourself.
- Run/swim/stretch/exercise/freshen up!
- Review all topics.
- Focus on a positive state of mind.
- Collect your thoughts.
- Breakfast – it's very important to make sure your body and brain have fuel.
- Check all your equipment, etc.

★ Your essential exam kit

Feeding your brain

For breakfast, have some cereal and fruit juice, and for lunch salads, fish and pasta are good.

If you are allowed to, take some water in a small plastic bottle into the exam with you, and even a few small chocolate bars and some fresh fruit, such as a banana, to boost energy between questions.

Equipment

Check you have enough pens, pencils, colours, rubber, ruler. Also – Maths equipment, calculator, any texts you're allowed, dictionary, lucky mascot and so on. Make sure your watch works and is accurate. Keep an eye on the exam hall clock and synchronise your watch with it.

Brain exercises

- Juggling or doodling with both hands will link both brain hemispheres and increase your concentration before you start the exam.
- There are neurovascular points on your head: on your forehead, behind your ears and around your temples which, when rubbed, will allow greater focus and concentration.
- Stretch, as if warming up for sport and gently roll your neck from side to side – not all the way around, as this can stretch it too much.

Stress

How to deal with it? If you're feeling under stress refer back to page 15 for ways to help yourself manage it.

Mental preparation

Your attitude/state of mind

- Smile!
- Think yourself in the exam ... ask typical questions: 'How would I answer ...?'
- Think of your past successes.
- Remember you know **much more** than you think you do.
- **Relax** and let the knowledge flow.
- Reaffirm venue and time of exams.

 Recognise that you should always remain calm to be at your best.

The exam

Examination tips and techniques

Set off for the exam after you've spent some time on mental preparation; get in the right frame of mind to tackle the work ahead. Take a brisk walk to the exam room and try to arrive about 5 minutes before the start. If you get there too early you'll have time to start feeling anxious; if you arrive later you'll feel rushed and unprepared.

Enter the exam room

- Check desk and chair; make sure they match to avoid rocking or discomfort.
- Set out your equipment.
- Focus on the future – what has motivated you all along?
- Relax and focus on the questions and topics you've practised.
- Try some more brain exercises – double doodles.
- Drink a little water.
- Smile (it helps everybody – but don't grin like an idiot!).
- Calm down … a few deep breaths.
- Be confident, think positively – believe in yourself.
- If in doubt about anything, ask the invigilator.

Follow instructions

- Listen to the invigilator. (There can be changes to instructions.)
- Read written instructions carefully, they will tell you: time; choice of questions; type of answer; number of marks.
- Fill in Examination Centre details and your name.
- Number the first page.
- Read all the questions. Eliminate those you don't want to do. Choose very carefully because each question deserves time – you may suddenly realise you **can** do it after all.
- Think about a general plan for the exam.
- Follow all instructions to the letter.

Planning your time

Read the questions – two to three times … slowly.

Remember how you've been advised to plan the exam

Reading time

Planning time

Time for each answer

Checking time

Draw up a plan – perhaps a pie chart

An example of how to plan your exam time

> Plan
> 9.15–9.30   Read, choose and plan
> 9.30–10.00   Question 1
> 10.00–10.30   Question 2
> 10.30–11.00   Question 3
> 11.00–11.30   Question 4
> 11.30–11.45   Check
> Total: 2½hours!

What happens if you don't plan your time?

- You rush answers and panic.
- You leave answers or miss obvious questions.
- Your memory doesn't react – so you begin to feel worried.

What happens if you fall behind in your plan?

- Don't panic: reduce each answer time – you **can** do it!
- Go into note form if absolutely necessary.
- Try to finish **each** question – show your working out if you have to.

Tackling the answers

You should have had plenty of practice at this!

- The type of plan doesn't matter. You can use: patterned notes, spidergrams, flow diagrams, paragraph headings or linear plans.
- You need to plan how much time you can devote to each answer. Allow time for **checking**.
- Plan in quiet reflection time between questions. A couple of minutes to take stock will help you maintain focus, concentration and allow you to unwind a little.
- Look for **key words** in questions – command and guide words. What does the examiner want?
- Look back at the section on written assignments (page 38). You should concentrate on: **Introduction**, **Development** and **Conclusion**.
- Try to put your points in an ordered, logical way (planning the answer will help with this).
- While sticking to your time plan and action plan you also need to relax and write freely – let it flow.
- If you are allowed to, drink some water every now and again.
- If eating is permitted, boost your energy with a banana or mini Mars.
- Stretches and brain exercises (page 14) can help your flow and release tension.

What is a 'good answer'?

A good answer ...

> comes from a well-revised topic
> is the result of a well-understood question
> is often anticipated in revision
> is planned carefully
> is relevant – and answers the question
> is clearly written and makes sense
> is presented well
> is produced in the way you've been taught
> is concluded and is checked
> pleases you!

What happens if your mind goes blank?

Panic and anxiety only lessens your chances of choosing the right question/point, so focus on being calmer and try to clear your head.

- Relaxation techniques do help.
- Massage the neurovascular points on your forehead.
- Focus your breathing: deep breaths.
- Don't spend too long trying to remember a point – leave a space or a line. Come back to it later.
- Keep writing. Jot any ideas or thoughts on rough paper.
- Ask yourself questions, then try again.

 *Remember – you **do** know it. If it's a very difficult question relax and resolve to give your best. Once you are calmer it is amazing how you will suddenly remember the information you need.*

In between exams if you have two on one day

- Get some fresh air – and move around.
- A possible plan is:

  Lunch – 20 minutes.

  Switch off – 15 minutes.

  Freshen up. Swim, shower – dunk head in water!

  Try focused review for 30 minutes.
- Relax. Remember ... **you can cope**.
- Treat the afternoon as a 'new day'.

Post mortems

Is a 'post mortem' a good idea?

Should you go through an exam immediately afterwards to assess your success rate?
The advantages are that you will have plenty of reassurance if you've done well!
The disadvantages are potentially dangerous – if you discover you've done badly, you will be highly demotivated and it will affect your other exams.

 Concentrate on the future – not the past, put it all down to experience and use your knowledge to help you next time.

Practical Exam Skills

PLAN YOUR TIME...

LOOK AT OLD PAPERS

USE ACTIVE REVISION

YOU CAN STILL IMPROVE!

ON THE DAY!

USE POSITIVE THINKING

YOU CAN DO IT!
BELIEVE IN YOURSELF!
YOU KNOW MORE
THAN YOU THINK!

GET UP EARLY...

DO SOME EXERCISE... EAT BREAKFAST... LEAVE ON TIME... KEEP CALM...

GET COMFORTABLE...

READ QUESTION 3 TIMES... PLAN ANSWER...

AND PASS!!!

Action plan

Go back to each section and pick ideas, suggestions and techniques that appeal to you. Then create at least **three objectives** that you intend to achieve from that section. So, for example, for *Your amazing brain power* on pages 2–5, one of your objectives might be:

- *I intend to learn using multisensory skills, including my visual, auditory and practical ones.*

Part One Your Amazing Brain

Your amazing brain power

1. . . . .

2. . . . .

3. . . . .

Multisensory learning

1. . . . .

2. . . . .

3. . . . .

Mind power

1. . . . .

2. . . . .

3. . . . .

Mind and body fitness

1. . . . .

2. . . . .

3. . . . .

Part Two Practical and Immediate Revision Skills

Environment, equipment and resources

1. . . . .

2. . . . .

3. . . . .

Organising time and mind

1. . . . .

2. . . . .

3. . . . .

What is memory?

1. . . . .

2. . . . .

3. . . . .

Reading and learning

1. . . . .

2. . . . .

3. . . . .

Listening skills

1. . . . .

2. . . . .

3. . . . .

Note taking

1. . . . .

2. . . . .

3. . . . .

Ideal revision

1. . . . .

2. . . . .

3. . . . .

Written answers

1. . . . .

2. . . . .

3. . . . .

Different types of questions

1. . . . .

2. . . . .

3. . . . .

Part Three Practical Exam Skills

Exam preparation

1. . . . .

2. . . . .

3. . . . .

The exam

1. . . . .

2. . . . .

3. . . . .

LONGMAN
BRAIN
TRAINERS

REVISION PLANNER

- As you revise, are you linking both sides of your brain?
- Are you employing all of your senses?
- Are you organised, and not distracted?
- Are you getting enough sleep, the right food and correct level of hydration?
- Do you have all the equipment you need?

Other study aids series available from Addison Wesley Longman:

Longman Study Guides (GCSE and A-level)
Longman Exam Practice Kits (GCSE and A-level)
Longman Practice Exam Papers (GCSE and A-level)
York Notes (GCSE and equivalent levels)
York Notes Advanced (A-level and above)

Find us on the web:
http://www.awl-he.com/studyguides

No. of weeks before the exams	Date: Week commencing	MONDAY	TUESDAY	WEDNESDAY	THURSDAY	FRIDAY	SATURDAY	SUNDAY
10								
9								
8								
7								
6								
5								
4								
3								
2								
1								

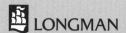